You'd Be So Pretty If . . .

You'd Be So Pretty If . . .

Teaching Our Daughters to Love Their Bodies—Even When We Don't Love Our Own

DARA CHADWICK

Da Capo

LIFE
LONG

A Member of the Perseus Books Group

Designed by Trish Wilkinson
Set in 12 point Goudy by the Perseus Books Group

Cataloging-in-Publication data for this book is
available from the Library of Congress.

First Da Capo Press edition 2009
ISBN: 978-07382-1258-6

Published by Da Capo Press
A Member of the Perseus Books Group
www.dacapopress.com

Note: The information in this book is true and complete to the best of our knowledge. This book is intended only as an informative guide for those wishing to know more about health issues. In no way is this book intended to replace, countermand, or conflict with the advice given to you by your own physician. The ultimate decision concerning care should be made between you and your doctor. We strongly recommend you follow his or her advice. Information in this book is general and is offered with no guarantees on the part of the authors or Da Capo Press. The authors and publisher disclaim all liability in connection with the use of this book. The names and identifying details of people associated with events described in this book have been changed. Any similarity to actual persons is coincidental.

10 9 8 7 6 5 4 3 2 1

For my mother, Jane
Forever in my heart, mind, and mirror

Author's Note

Some of the names in this book have been changed to protect the privacy of the many women and girls who so graciously shared their stories with me.

Contents

PART 4
Full Circle

Introduction

I grew up listening to my mom bemoan everything from the size of her thighs to the shape of her eyes. So you can imagine my dismay the first time someone exclaimed, "You look just like your mother!"

It wasn't that I thought she wasn't beautiful—it was that I knew *she* thought she wasn't beautiful. So if I looked like her, and she didn't like the way she looked, then that must mean . . .

You see where I'm going with this, right?

For years, dissatisfaction with my body simmered beneath my skin like a low-grade fever. Never bad enough to keep me from going about the business of my life— dating, working, getting married, having children—but always present enough to keep me from feeling my best. I'd go to the beach but refuse to strip down to my bathing suit, choosing instead to just wet my feet at the water's edge in my shorts and T-shirt. I'd go to parties but hang back, wishing I had the confidence of the other women there, all of whom I imagined were completely happy with the way they looked. I wasn't having a body image crisis so much as I was feeling what I've come to realize many women feel—a nagging sense of "If only . . ." If only I were taller. If only my thighs weren't so rounded. If only . . .

Fast-forward now about fifteen years. After two pregnancies and a decade of bad habits, I'm overweight and unhappy with the way I look and feel. In 2007, I stumbled on the opportunity to become the Weight-Loss Diary columnist for *Shape*, a women's fitness magazine. I wrote a surprisingly passionate email to the editor about why I wanted to lose twenty-five pounds—how I wanted to feel healthy and strong and, most importantly, how I wanted to set a good example for my then eleven-year-old daughter, Faith. Writing that email brought something out in me, and to my delight and terror I was chosen for the column.

Each month for a year, I wrote about practical weight-loss issues like healthy eating, working out, and managing food temptations. Every column required a photo shoot and a dreaded weigh-in and body fat measure. Working with a team of professionals chosen for me by the magazine—a personal trainer, a dietitian, and a life coach—I reshaped my body with a six-days-a-week program of strength training and cardio workouts. I learned to eat a diet of mostly vegetables, lean proteins, and healthy carbohydrates. And perhaps most importantly, I learned to face the psychological challenges—guilt, fear, self-judgment—that kept me from taking good care of myself and my health. Through it all, I agonized over the effect that the project was having on my daughter. I hated revealing my weight—a number I *never* talked about—to the world. But mostly, I worried that seeing me obsess about calories and gym time and body fat numbers would teach my daughter that this is normal female behavior. Would she think that if this is what Mom worries about, she should worry about it, too?

So we talked—a lot. We talked about why I wanted to do the *Shape* project, what it meant (no, I didn't hate myself, but I wanted to feel better), and what my ultimate goal was (to live a healthy, confident life). In the end, the column was a gift in ways I never imagined. Yes, the year of personal training, life coaching, and nutrition counseling helped me shed twenty-six pounds and take control of my lifestyle. But more important, the entire experience—all the hours in the gym, meetings with the nutritionist, all the exploring of my feelings about my body, and even the year of professional photo shoots—sparked many conversations between me and my girl. What we got, together, was a crash course in what can and can't be changed, how the media can manipulate what's real and what isn't, and how what we say to ourselves *about* ourselves is what really matters.

Readers watched my transformation each month, but it was the column I wrote for the May 2007 issue that sparked the idea for this book. In it, I reflected on how my mother's feelings about her body had affected my feelings about mine, and how my feelings were shaping my daughter's feelings about her body. It was the first time I'd ever really stopped to consider my body image legacy—or the legacy I was creating for my girl. It was a topic that struck a chord with many readers.

Digging into my body image past was an uncomfortable experience. I have many a memory of cringing in department store dressing rooms as my mom pointed out her flaws to total strangers. "This one'll hide a multitude of sins," she'd say, holding up a shirt two sizes too big. She had a wicked sense of humor, and jokes at her own expense were always her favorite; she made coworkers howl with cracks like, "The first rich blind man through the door is mine." Sure, after three kids, little exercise, and not the greatest dietary habits, she was a bit overweight. But we're only talking a size 12 or 14 on a five-foot-two frame.

Over time, her self-deprecating habits became my own, and her body feelings became mine. Plenty of jokes have been written about the moment when a woman discovers she's turned into her mother. Mine came about a week after my mother died. My sister-in-law handed me a framed photo of my mother and me, taken about six months earlier at our family's Christmas gathering. In it, we're wearing the exact same outfit: black pants and long red sweaters that reached down past our hips. I know she was thinking the same thing I was when I got dressed that day: black on the bottom to minimize, something long and shapeless on the top so no one will know what's underneath.

That was the day it hit me—just how much power I have in shaping my daughter's future relationship with her body.

The Body Image Legacy

When I started writing this book, I thought it was going to be about making peace with the body baggage my mother had handed off to me—and about making peace with her. But it isn't. It's about changing the body image legacy I leave to my daughter. And the one you leave to yours.

I'd always tried hard not to criticize my body in front of her. I didn't want her to see herself in me—as I saw myself in my mother—and think that I didn't like what she saw in the mirror. My theory was always that if I didn't say it out loud, my self-criticisms wouldn't become hers when her thighs inevitably began to take on the family shape.

Now, at thirteen, my daughter is nothing short of amazing. She's smart, and she doesn't care who knows it. She's obsessed with softball; from the bleachers, I watch her mouth set in determination as she gets under a fly ball that she quickly turns into a double play. I watch her skip up the street with her friends, her ponytail swinging behind her, and just for a moment, it takes my breath away. I hope she'll always be like this—confident and comfortable in her own skin.

But already, trouble is brewing. It's in the piles of clothes on her bedroom floor, left there when she's tried on outfit after outfit. It's in the way she adjusts the straps of her tank top and smoothes her skirt when she catches a glimpse of herself in a window. Her body is beginning to change, and she's not sure what to make of it. The powerful legs that round the bases toward home plate are suddenly "too big" in her eyes. And it's in these moments that it hits me: I wasn't nearly as skilled at hiding my feelings as I thought. These feelings—that harsh inner critic that curses the family curves—are my legacy to her, just as they were my mother's legacy to me.

The way girls feel about their bodies has consequences that reach far beyond simply how they react when they look in the mirror. How they feel about the way they *look* often has a direct effect on how they feel about who they *are*. According to *Real Girls, Real Pressure: A National Report on the State of Self-Esteem*, commissioned by the Dove Self-Esteem Fund in June 2008, 75 percent of girls between the ages of eight and seventeen with low self-esteem reported engaging in harmful activities like bullying, smoking, drinking, and cutting themselves. Another 25 percent of girls with low self-esteem admitted to starving themselves, refusing to eat, or binging and throwing up.

As moms, we should know that our own body image past deeply affects how our girls feel about their bodies today. The good news, though, is that it's not too late to change that legacy. Anyone who's had a mother or is a mother—and that's all of us—knows the power that Mom has. In fact, according to the Dove report, 67 percent of girls ages thirteen to seventeen turn to their mother when they're feeling bad about themselves—and 91 percent of girls ages eight to twelve do. Clearly, moms are important. We can criticize with a glance, scold with a sigh, or shatter with a single word. But we can also encourage with a smile, compliment with a look, and serve as role models with the choices we make for ourselves. It really is that simple. How I treat my body today—what I choose to feed it, how I choose to make it work, how I dress it, and, perhaps most important, how I talk about it—has a profound effect on how my daughter will treat her own body tomorrow.

Why It Matters

Sure, it's important for our daughters to know that they're smart and that they're capable and that they can accomplish anything. But all the smarts in the world don't matter if a girl refuses to raise her hand in class because she's afraid her classmates will look at her and find her appearance lacking. A woman can be incredibly capable, yet if she won't give a presentation or step forward to be considered for a promotion because she feels "too fat" to stand up in front of a group, her capabilities will never be recognized. Body image matters not because we all need to look like gorgeous supermodels to be happy. It matters because if we don't feel good about what we look like and the body we live in, we're less inclined to show the world who we are.

That world may be full of influences that are beyond our control, but the reality is this: As mothers, how we feel about and relate to our own bodies—and the conscious or unconscious expression of that relationship—creates a "body image blueprint" for our daughters. Our girls may grow up to look different from the way we look, but the foundation for how they relate to their bodies as adults is one that we help to build, brick by brick, through our behavior toward our own bodies and toward theirs.

Lead by Example

I wanted this book to be different from all the other body image books out there. I didn't want to write another book about how we should all join hands and embrace ourselves, our flaws, and each other. It's a nice sentiment, but I think we all know it's not happening anytime soon. Instead, I wanted to write about how mothers can change things for their girls—and, ultimately, themselves—not with grand gestures, but with little tweaks that have big effects. This book is about being a positive example for your daughter, even if your own body is far from what you wish it was. You don't have to look like a supermodel to do it, I promise.

Throughout this book, you'll learn to reflect on the body image "blueprint" you inherited from your mother and how to change—or reinforce—the way you teach your daughter to see her own body. You'll find expert advice on teaching your daughter about healthy eating, how to have a healthy relationship with exercise, how to keep the number on the scale in perspective, and how to compare herself in a healthy way to media images and to girls and women in her own life. You'll also learn about the effects that males (whether brothers, boyfriends, or fathers) can have on your daughter's body image, as well as what to do if you think your daughter might have an eating disorder. Through it all, you'll read expert advice, personal reflections, and lessons learned from women and moms who've been right where you are.

You'll find lots of stories in this book, not just mine but those of the many women and girls I interviewed while researching. Some are heartbreaking, some will make you laugh, and some will make you say, "Why didn't I think of that?" But they'll all teach you the most important thing you need to know to raise a daughter who feels good about herself: she's watching you and listening to what you say. The message is up to you.

PART 1

Birth of a Body Image

Carry My Bags
Understanding Your Body Image History

> I talk to my mom about my thighs, and she says
> she doesn't like her thighs, too. . . . she says all
> Italians have fat thighs.
>
> —*Laurie, age ten*

It was a moment of what I can only describe as desperation. I was traveling to a writing conference in New York City the following week, and I needed a new outfit to wear during my scheduled meetings with editors. I'd grown accustomed to my daily in-home office uniform of baggy jeans and oversized sweaters. I felt most comfortable if I hid my post-baby body, which had grown ever larger over the years as regular exercise and healthy eating fell to the bottom of my priority list. But as I stood in the tiny cubicle of a dressing room at a local department store, armed with skirts, blouses, and pants, I was determined to leave that store with something—*anything*—that made me look like the competent professional I was.

I should have known better than to leave this task until the last minute. Though I rarely took my daughter, Faith, with me when I shopped for my own clothes, we'd gone out together that day. She sat in a corner of the cubicle, watching as I tried on skirts and blouses. Nothing was right. I slipped on a black skirt and frowned as I turned to look at my backside. "Nope," I said. "This one's too tight."

So I tried another. "That looks good, Mom," she said as I buttoned a navy skirt around my waist.

"No," I told her, trying to smooth down the front. "See how it pulls? It's because my hips are so much bigger than my waist."

Frustrated, I pulled the skirt off and grabbed a pair of pants. They fit fine around the hips, but there was such a gap at the waist, somebody else could have gotten in with me.

"You could get a belt," Faith offered, trying to be helpful.

"No," I practically hissed. "They're way too big in the waist. And a belt would look weird. And it's too late now to have them altered."

Finally, I grabbed a black pantsuit from a hanger. As I buttoned the jacket, Faith said, "That looks really good, Mom." It did look decent, I suppose; the fit was tolerable, and it was certainly professional enough. But it didn't look the way I wanted it to look—because my body didn't look the way I wanted it to look. In that moment, I knew no suit in the world was going to make my body right in my eyes. But how could I say that to my daughter? And, really, instinct told me I *shouldn't* say that to my daughter. Here she was trying to help, not a body concern of her own in the world, really thinking that I did look good in the suit. She didn't need to hear this from me.

"You should get it, Mom," she said. "It looks really nice."

"You know what, honey?" I told her. "It's kind of expensive. I think I'll just wear something I already have."

I turned away so she wouldn't see the tears welling up in my eyes as I took off the suit. I'd just flashed back to a memory of my own mother.

~

I was twenty-four years old, and my mother had taken me shopping with her when she was looking for a dress to wear to my brother's wedding. She'd grown increasingly frustrated looking for something she called "decent" during the previous few weeks, but she was determined to find something that day. She went into the dressing room and tried on a purple two-piece suit that I'd found on a rack. She was skeptical—she never wore fitted jackets, and she wasn't a huge fan of purple—but I pushed her to try it on, and when she did, I thought it looked lovely. The cut of the jacket created a nice waistline, and the color was so pretty against her skin and her dark hair.

"I don't know," she'd said doubtfully.

"Buy it," I told her. "It looks really nice."

She bought the suit and wore it—beautifully, I thought. But months later, when we shopped for her mother-of-the-bride dress for my own wedding, she chose a pale green dress with a big swath of cloth that draped across the middle. "I never liked that purple suit," she told me. "I let you talk me into it, and I felt awful in it. This is better. No one can tell what's under it."

Her words stung. Didn't she know how nice I thought she looked that day? I'd certainly told her, and I wouldn't lie to her. But my words didn't matter, and I should have known that they wouldn't. I can't ever remember my mother receiving a compliment about her appearance that she didn't quickly brush off. Growing up, I was well aware of the fact that she didn't like the way her body looked—and other people's words to the contrary were simply not to be believed.

It was a lesson I internalized early. My whole life, I listened to her criticize her own rounded middle. To Mom, loose-fitting clothes were a means to hide the flaws she saw in her figure; the excess weight she carried was a source of shame. She rarely bought new clothes for herself, preferring instead to hide under big T-shirts. And she refused to wear shorts, much less a swimsuit, even on the hottest days of the summer. She was too ashamed of what she thought were her less-than-perfect, "sticklike" legs.

I *hated* hearing her talk like that. And I hated seeing her hold back—sweltering in jeans in the heat of summer, never going for a swim, not graciously accepting a compliment on a dress that everyone else thought looked lovely on her. After all, she may have been carrying a few extra pounds in places, but she wasn't obese; she probably weighed about 150 pounds. Still, my mother always told me, "If you think you're fat, you are."

If you think you're fat, you are. Those words echoed in my head as I left the store with Faith that day.

"Mom, how come you never buy anything for yourself?" she asked as we walked to the car.

"I don't know," I lied. "I'd rather spend money on you and Evan."

I smiled at her, and she smiled back. But something in her eyes told me she already knew the truth—and I suddenly imagined her in a store dressing room with *her* daughter someday, remembering my unwillingness to treat my "imperfect" body to something new and struggling to appreciate her own because of my example.

I didn't want that for her. But after years of believing that only girls and women with "good" bodies—you know, the ones that lacked the flaws I saw in my own—were entitled to show off their figures with stylish new clothes, I wasn't sure how to change my behavior.

It wasn't long after that incident in the store dressing room that I was presented with the opportunity to write *Shape* magazine's Weight-Loss Diary column. Here was my chance, I thought. I'd finally take off the extra pounds I'd packed on and whip my body into the best shape it had ever been in. It was an incredible opportunity, but I worried about the effect it might have on me. I'd flirted with an eating disorder as a teenager, and the prospect of tapping into those feelings again—that delicious power you feel when the pounds come off—scared me a bit. I wasn't sure I could trust myself not to go down that road, and I knew I didn't want my daughter to see me like that. But in spite of my fears, something told me I should do this, that I should make every attempt to conquer my body demons so that my daughter could see what it was like to be a grown woman who liked what she saw in the mirror.

I also knew that losing weight was about much more than my vanity. I'd lost my mother three years earlier. At just sixty years old, her medical problems weren't based in weight, although carrying extra pounds certainly didn't help her health. But her early death (and that of her mother at the age of sixty-three) was a constant reminder to me about the value—and the fragility—of good health. As a grown woman and a mom, losing weight wasn't just about looking better for me; it was about trying to be around long enough to play with my grandchildren.

Mom Sets the Stage

I find it pretty ironic that the very thing I was so conscious of while growing up—the fact that my mom didn't like the way her body looked—still managed to play itself out in my own behavior when I became an adult. During my year writing *Shape*'s Weight-Loss Diary, I worked with a life coach, Pavitra Ciavardone, whose job it was to help me address some of the psychological barriers that were standing between me and weight loss. I worried that exploring some of these barriers would be all about blaming others, something I didn't want to do. My issues were my own. But as I reflected on my relationship with my mom, what I had to acknowledge was that, yes, I had been shaped by her feelings about her body, just as she had been shaped by those of her mother. (My maternal grandmother died when I was just three, but I know my mother grew up feeling that thinking too much of yourself was a great character flaw. My grandmother referred to her own shape as a "barrel on two sticks" and often criticized her rounded middle.) I soon realized acknowledging that body feelings often travel down the generational chain wasn't about blaming but about understanding—an understanding that helped me see I could choose to let go of the body image "lessons" I had learned.

Although there's no denying the magnetic pull of the patterns and behaviors we learn in childhood, we aren't destined to automatically pick up the body baggage that our mothers carried. Recognize the power you have as a mother in molding your daughter's self-image. What you say about her body and about your own will ultimately help shape her adult feelings about who she is.

"Mom is the rule," says Dr. Laura Jana, a pediatrician and author of *Food Fights*. "Yes, the media and magazines and all those things can have a very big impact on body image. But as your daughter's mother, you have the potential to have an even bigger impact."

According to Melissa Kirdzik, a registered dietitian (my dietitian during the Weight-Loss Diary column), you can lay the groundwork for a healthy body image in your girl by conveying feelings, not judgments, about your own body. "Instead of saying, 'I look fat,' it's better to say, 'I don't like how I feel,'" she says. So when I took on the Weight-Loss Diary, I tried to help Faith understand that my wanting to lose weight wasn't about wanting to look like somebody else. We talked about good health and the fact that getting to a lower weight was healthier for someone my height. But I knew I had to be honest with her about the whole picture, too. I told her that growing up, I'd always felt like my mom wasn't comfortable in her own skin and that because she wasn't comfortable, it made her sad. I told her I felt sad sometimes, too, because I didn't feel that I was the best me I could be. She seemed surprised; to her, I'm just Mom, and she thinks I'm beautiful because she loves me. But I explained that it's how I *feel* that's important—and it was important to me to feel healthy and good again.

A Link in the Chain

Talk to just about any woman, and you'll quickly find that she has a mother (or grandmother) story when it comes to body image. After all, our moms teach us what being a woman is all about, including the importance— or unimportance—of our appearance. "I think my mom hated her body," says thirty-five-year-old Traci. "To her, appearance seemed to be everything. If someone popped in on us and her hair was in a scarf, she wouldn't answer the door. She'd have us hide and be quiet."

Traci tells me her mom's example has definitely played itself out in her own life. "I've skipped parties because I didn't feel good about myself," she says. "And I didn't tell the fitness instructors or personal trainers at the gym that I was working on my personal trainer certification be-cause I'm still a little embarrassed that I don't have a six-pack or superthin thighs. I didn't want them to think, 'Are you kidding? You, a personal trainer?'"

Traci's certainly not alone in her experience. Whether your mother felt great about her body or hated everything about the way she looked, you can bet that her example played a powerful role in shaping how you feel about your body today. It's no different when it comes to you and your daughter.

Nancy, age forty-one, knows all too well what it's like to grow up with a mom who hates her body. Her mom dieted constantly and controlled what Nancy and her sister ate, too, for fear that they'd "get fat." For years, Nancy watched her mother punish herself with four-hour workouts and a fasting program that sometimes had her eating only on weekends. During puberty, Nancy began to put on weight herself, and by her freshman year of high school, Nancy—who remembers wearing a size 8 or 10 then—was begging her mother to send her to a weight-loss camp that she'd found in the back of a teen magazine. Her mother agreed. "At that point in time, a little bit of chub and you were fat," she says, reflecting on the fact that her mother would agree to send her to a weight-loss camp when she wore a size 8. "My mother was always on a diet; she was always measuring or watching. When I look at pictures of myself from high school now—I mean, I was overweight, but I wasn't big by any stretch of the imagination. But I considered myself completely un-dateable, and I pinned all my self-esteem on somebody else's opinion of me." It was an opinion that Nancy carried with her for years.

Today, Nancy sees the absurdity in thinking that at a size 8 she was too big. She once questioned her mother about why she'd been so critical of her weight and controlling of what she ate. Her mother's answer was simple: "You weren't heavy then, but I wanted to keep you from getting heavy."

Dealing with the Legacy You Inherited

Understanding our role in shaping our daughters' body image can be a painful process because we're forced to examine our own body image legacy—particularly if that legacy wasn't positive.

"I never realized how much power you have as a parent," Carolyn, age forty-eight, tells me, recounting that more than any other lesson, her mother taught her that it was "bad" to be fat. "I never really got that until I had my own kid." Today, Carolyn says she works hard to shield her twelve-year-old daughter, who struggles with her weight, from insensitive comments that the older generation of her family will sometimes make. "I've forbidden all discussion of her weight," she says. "There's no teasing, no pinching, no nothing."

Many adult daughters have a moment of recognition in which they see a glimpse of the girl their mother once was. Sometimes it's witnessing an exchange between your mom and your grandmother, and getting a truer sense of the dynamic your mother lived with as a daughter. Sometimes it's hearing your mom share a painful memory from her own adolescence and suddenly knowing that the pain of that experience has colored her exchanges with you. Or it's simply coming to understand the vulnerability that harsh self-criticism—or criticism of you—often masks. These moments of recognition can help to heal stormy mother-and-daughter relationships. They can also give us a greater window into understanding the foundation of our own body image.

Taking on the *Shape* project was my attempt to get things moving in the right direction for Faith—and for me. I wanted her to see me commit to taking care of my body. I wanted her to see me healthy, strong, and proud of it, not miserable about everything my body wasn't. But mostly, I wanted to reconcile my own feelings about my body so that I wouldn't hand them off to her.

It's not always easy; you can't just snap your fingers and make habits you've lived with for years simply disappear. But it's not as difficult as you might think, either. It's about recognizing the moments when a subtle shift— a slightly different choice—will make all the difference to your daughter—and to you.

Fake It 'til You Make It

We can't control what we look like, but we can change our attitude about it.

No, it's not always easy to model positive body image behavior in front of your kids. Sometimes, it takes a bit of "fake it 'til you make it." Even after I lost twenty-six pounds and dropped four sizes, there are still parts of my body that I don't necessarily like the look of. But I have been making an effort not to fixate on changing those parts. I still have my dressing room moments, but these days, I'm much more likely to blame the clothes than I am to blame my body. Instead of saying, "Ugh, my thighs are enormous" when I'm trying on pants that don't fit well, I'll say, "I'm going to try another pair that's more flattering." It's a subtle shift, but one that doesn't fail to register with a girl who's listening.

And rest assured, our girls are always listening. They're watching, too.

Take fifteen-year-old Grace, for example. "My mom wants to lose twenty pounds, which I find ridiculous because she's perfect the way she is," Grace tells me. "I don't see why she wants to lose weight. I just wish she could see her body the way everyone else does."

When I ask Grace what makes a girl pretty, she says, "Confidence." And she gets mad when her mom thinks she lacks it. "I hate it when my mom says things without thinking," she tells me. "She thinks I'm uncomfortable with my body, too, but I'm really fine with it." Right now, Grace says she doesn't have any hang-ups about the way she looks. But sometimes, a mom's attention and focus on her own figure flaws can make her daughter second-guess herself.

That's a trap a lot of us moms fall into. We sometimes have trouble separating our own painful memories and feelings from what our daughters are experiencing. We project our feelings onto our girls, and we imagine that our struggles will become their struggles unless we step in to stop it. With our own pain so close to the surface, it's all too easy to adopt an extreme approach to sparing our girls from what we imagine will be the same fate. But simply put, that's not our job. Better we should focus on addressing our own body issues so that we can show our girls what a healthy relationship with their bodies should look like.

According to Amber Rickert, MSW, MPH, a clinical social worker who works with adolescents, faking body confidence in front of your daughter is a good thing. Modeling is extremely important for adolescents, she tells me, adding that it's crucial for girls to hear adults talking about their bodies in a positive way and treating their bodies well—even if the adults might not exactly be feeling the love inside.

"You can go deconstruct your body all you want when you're by yourself," she says. "But if you're constantly deconstructing it in front of her, she's going to absorb that."

Making an effort to point out what's good about your body in front of your daughter—even if you don't necessarily *believe* it—and treating your body well are good not only for you but for your girl, too. You don't have to pretend to love everything about the way you look—I certainly don't love everything about the way I look—but remember that your words and actions are affecting her, even when they're not aimed at her. Understanding that distinction is what makes the difference in the kind of body image role models we'll be for our daughters—and they'll be for theirs.

Body Image Builders

We all carry our own body image legacy from childhood to adulthood. Recognizing and making peace with that legacy are the first steps in changing the message we send to our daughters about our bodies—and about theirs. Consider this advice when reflecting on how you feel about your body:

Know your own history. Think about the "body image blueprint" you grew up with. It's good to know where you're coming from so you can make conscious choices about the messages you send to your daughter.

Respect your body's wisdom. The body you're in today isn't the same one you grew up in. It may have given birth, survived an accident or an illness, or carried you through difficult times. You wouldn't trade the lessons you've learned or the wisdom you've gained from those experiences, so give your body permission to reflect the changes it's been through.

Change your tune. If you're usually harsh or critical about your body or appearance in front of your daughter, make sure she hears you say at least one positive thing about yourself each day. A simple "I like the way my hair looks today" or "I like the cut of these pants" is a great first step toward creating a more positive body image.

Take a compliment. When someone says something nice about the way you look, don't be so quick to brush it off, especially if your daughter is watching. You may not agree with the compliment, but a simple "Thanks" is all you need to say.

Give a compliment—to yourself. Just as it's important for your daughter to hear you graciously accept a compliment, it's also important for her to hear you give yourself one. It's not bragging to say something positive about yourself, and it teaches her that it's OK to see the good in herself, not just the "flaws."

It's a Girl!

Her Body Image Starts with Yours

> I pay attention to what my mom says. When she relates situations to real-life stories, it makes me think. But I really do think she says I'm pretty because she's my mom.
>
> —*Allison, age twelve*

From the moment her daughter is born, just about every woman is clear on two things—all the ways she hopes her daughter will grow up to be just like her and all the ways she hopes things will be different for her girl. When I think about being a body image "role model" for Faith, I confess I sometimes feel anxious. I'm confident that I can show her how to be smart and organized, how to go after her dreams, how to be a loving mom who takes good care of home, friends, and family. These are all areas where I feel I know my stuff. But show her how to feel great about her body and how it looks?

Not so much.

When Faith was little, I used to read a ton of parenting books and magazines. It was practically an obsession; I was always searching for expert advice on what I needed to do so my baby would grow up healthy and happy. I was always looking for strategies for handling the latest "challenge" of being a mom. Somewhere in the first few months of her life, Faith developed a severe case of colic. Every afternoon, she'd scream for about three hours straight, so much so that I thought I might lose my mind. I frantically searched for strategies to outsmart colic, but there was no surefire cure. On one especially trying afternoon, when I'd driven and rocked and swaddled and sung until I could do no more, I called my mother at work and cried. She heard the desperation in my voice and said, "Dara, you need to calm down. The more anxious you are, the more anxious she'll be."

She was right. I took a deep breath and surrendered to the moment, and things improved almost instantly. It was my first real-world experience with understanding just how strong an effect my behavior and attitude have on my daughter.

They're Never Too Young to Learn

As adults, we tend to think that kids aren't paying attention and that what we say to ourselves or each other in hushed tones goes right over their heads. Of course, if you've ever heard a toddler repeat a questionable word at a most inopportune moment—like when you're outside chatting with your elderly neighbor, for instance—you probably already know that kids are soaking up our example much earlier than we think. Little girls have long raided their mothers' jewelry boxes and makeup kits, trying to be just like Mom. I can remember Faith begging me to put curlers in her hair at the age of three; she'd seen me using hot rollers while getting ready for a wedding and wanted her hair to be "so beautiful," too.

Toddlers and preschoolers are little imitators, and they're quick to pick up on the behaviors they see and the comments they hear. When she's young, your daughter's behavior is all about pleasing you. That's exactly how I found myself suffering the indignity of a perm at the hands of my mother in the family kitchen when I was just seven years old. Though I was certainly curious about why my fine, straight hair wasn't OK the way it was, I wanted to make her happy, and if curly hair would do that, then I was willing to sit through the stinky mess. After all, what did I care? I'd rather be climbing fences and having stick-sword fights with the neighborhood boys. Now I just looked like a poodle while doing it.

As moms, we set the tone in teaching our girls about appearance and what it means. Karin, age forty-eight, was thrilled to give birth to a baby girl just as the second of her two sons was heading off to kindergarten. She filled the nursery closet with pink and had visions of dressing her little princess in ladylike tights, dresses, and hair bows. But Amanda, who's now thirteen, had other ideas. Though Karin tried to dress Amanda like a pretty doll, by the time she was a toddler, Amanda preferred overalls and rolling around on the floor with her older brothers.

"I always liked to fix her hair, and she didn't like to have her hair fixed," Karin tells me. "She didn't like to shop. It was all very frustrating to me." Ultimately, Karin says, she had to let go and let Amanda be just who she is.

But letting go is so hard, isn't it?

I imagine there's not a woman reading this who can't remember at least one time when her mom forced her to wear something she remembers as truly horrific (for me, it was a fake-fur white hood that buttoned under the chin, which prompted my brothers to call me a sheep and make "baa" noises whenever I wore it). When we insist that our daughters look a certain way—whether it's what they wear, how their hair looks, or how they have to behave in what they're wearing—we're building the foundation for how they see their bodies and the importance of how they look.

When I became a mom myself, I soon learned that although my little girl wanted to please me, she also had a mind of her own. She liked to choose her own outfits and preferred dresses; she balked at the adorable little matching pants-and-shirts combinations I picked out for her. My mother, an avid seamstress, had made a few jumpers for Faith, and Faith wanted to wear them *all* the time. My inner feminist worried that the dresses would interfere with her running, climbing, and playing. So we compromised: For almost a year, Faith wore a dress over her pants and shirt—even as she made mud pies in the backyard and wrestled with her brother. Somewhere, there's a great family photo of her in a football jersey and a white tutu. I love that picture. For me, it's the ultimate portrait of what being a little girl means—moving between the glamour of grown-up ladies and the rough-and-tumble action of exploring the world.

Who Wants to Grow Up?

Ever remember your mom telling you to "act like a lady"? I was at a kid's birthday party recently where a little girl in a beautiful frilly dress was enjoying the breeze she made as she spun and spun, her dress flying up, not a care in the world. I'll never forget the look on her face as her mother took her by the arm, told her to stop, and informed her that "nice girls don't do that."

Later, as the cake was cut, the grown-up women inevitably began to discuss calorie counts and how they "really shouldn't" have a piece. For the little girls in the room who were watching, the lesson was that "acting like a lady" means you don't get cake—not a whole lot of incentive to grow up there! Or if you do take a piece, being a grown-up lady means you spend the next twenty minutes talking about how you don't deserve cake because your thighs are already too big.

What's the real effect? I've been guilty of thinking that those kinds of comments go right over my daughter's head—or that she gets the "joke"—but the reality is our girls don't, especially if they hear us talking that way frequently. One isolated remark here or there about your body probably isn't going to damage your daughter, but when mothers repeatedly make negative comments about their bodies, it creates a model for how daughters feel about themselves, says Andrea Vazzana, PhD, a clinical psychologist practicing at the NYU Child Study Center. She's seen it play out in her practice: Mothers who constantly talk about their bodies send a message to their daughters that physical appearance is important. And when mothers talk about their dissatisfaction with their bodies, daughters can come to think that feeling bad about their bodies is the norm, putting them at higher risk for developing similar feelings and for making negative comments about their own bodies.

Telling your daughter that she's going to end up just like you—or worse, telling her that you *hope she doesn't* end up like you—is dangerous ground. "My nana is an overweight person, and she's always saying that boys won't be interested in me at all if I don't try to make myself as pretty as I can be," says Amanda, age thirteen. I've caught myself telling Faith that I hope she'll be taller than I am. What I was thinking was that being taller might mean she wouldn't have to work as hard to maintain a healthy weight and might have an easier time finding clothes that fit her well. What she heard, of course, was "being short isn't a good thing." And since height is a physical attribute that can't be changed, was I planting the seed for a lifetime of her feeling that she's "less than" for something she can't do anything about?

It might sound extreme, I know, but offhand comments like these and our own behavior toward our bodies have a profound effect on our girls. "My mom says her bum is too big," Kelly, age fourteen, says. "She exercises a lot, and she doesn't eat desserts. I hate it when she tells me *my* jeans are too tight."

Who among us can't remember a time when someone—if it wasn't a mom, maybe it was a grandma, an aunt, an uncle, or another "well-meaning" relative—said something that made us all of a sudden feel not quite right, often related to a body part that we supposedly "got" from someone else in the family? Ever been told you have your mom's distinctively rounded bottom or your grandma's knobby knees? I'm willing to bet you never looked at those body parts the same way after that.

When you fixate out loud on some physical part that you don't like about yourself, whether it's your thighs, your nose, your middle, or any body part you imagine to be your most grotesque flaw, you may be teaching your daughter that the whole package of "who we are" doesn't matter. Instead, we teach them to pick themselves apart and dissect their flaws as we've done to ourselves. We teach them to imagine that other people look at them and see only the things they don't like about themselves. And we teach them not to trust their own judgment about what beauty really is.

"I'm really self-conscious about certain things, and a lot of times I only talk about it with friends I have that sort of think the same thing about the way they look," says Amanda. "I would [like to] lose some weight. I mean, I wouldn't make myself super-skinny—just average-sized. Also, I'd want to be a bit shorter. I'm not a huge fan of how tall I am."

Brace Yourself: Here Comes Puberty

Ah, puberty. A time of fond memories for all of us, no? There's something unsettling about watching your daughter's body begin to change. Not only does it punctuate the fact that *we're* getting older, but it's also hard not to see yourself at that age and remember how it felt to watch your own body morph into something you don't quite recognize anymore. Sometimes I feel like a spectator, watching the young girl Faith was start to fade into the background as the woman she'll become begins to emerge.

According to Dr. Vazzana, kids become aware of their bodies as early as two years old, and by preschool they're well aware of how their different physical characteristics can be seen as negative or positive. In elementary school, kids are often teased about their weight, and peers start to make judgments about their bodies.

The very fact that the course of puberty is such an individual thing is part of what makes this time so tough to navigate for both moms and girls. Girls (and sometimes moms) get anxious about how their bodies compare to those of their friends and even their siblings. Physical attractiveness takes on a whole new importance as girls step into the intense middle-school world of peer pressure and, of course, boys.

Here's the bottom line: As your daughter enters puberty and her body begins to change, you should expect those changes might bring up not only some of your own painful memories of that time in your life, but also some of your own unresolved body image issues. If you've spent decades nursing body image wounds that began in your teenage years, don't be surprised if your feelings intensify when you start to see changes in your daughter's body. But there's a crucial fact we have to remember, says Dr. Vazzana. Girls, and moms, need to understand that weight gain is part of *normal* development in puberty. "Girls need to know that this is going to happen," she says. "They need to know that it's expected, and it's not something they should fear or be embarrassed about."

Traci, age thirty-five, vividly remembers her mother telling her that if she continued to eat as much as her dad, it would catch up with her, and she'd end up fat. "I remember hating my scrawny stork legs," she tells me. "Then I began to get curves, and by the time I was a junior, I thought my legs were fat. By senior year, I was drinking Slim Fast for lunch."

While it's certainly a good idea to encourage healthy eating and good food choices in our girls at any age, we have to know that we're tiptoeing along a very dangerous line here. As our daughters begin to gain weight, as they should, we have to squelch the impulse to do what we can to control that weight. For many moms, not wanting your daughter to gain weight isn't about not wanting her to grow up; it's about wanting her to stay in that place where she feels good about her body. It's an extremely difficult course to navigate, but our response to their weight gain makes a huge difference in how they feel about their bodies.

If we treat weight gain at puberty as something that must be avoided or carefully controlled—or, worse, is the result of something they've done wrong—the hurt we create is something that can't always be undone.

This can be a great time to share stories of your own adolescence, but only if your daughter wants to hear them. Faith loves to hear stories of my middle-school days; she seems most drawn to the ones in which I share how "different" I felt and how I struggled to find my place in the social structure of school. Girls this age often can't—or won't—talk to each other about their changing bodies and how they feel. That's where moms come in. A well-timed, relevant story lets your daughter know that she's not the only one who's ever felt like this, nor is she doomed to feel this way forever.

But remember, our behavior now has to match what we say we've learned from our own experiences. Many moms are coping with body changes of their own—changes from childbirth, illness, perimenopause, and menopause—just as their daughters are coping with the body changes of puberty (leading many dads to want to duck, cover, and run, I'm sure). We can tell our girls that they'll get through this tough time and that their bodies are just fine as they are, but if our behavior doesn't reflect what we're saying—if we're still putting our own bodies down constantly or endlessly trying to diet down to a weight that's no longer realistic for the body we have today—our stories quickly lose credibility with our girls.

As our girls become more aware of their bodies—and of all the ways they're different from their friends—it's more important than ever for us to rein in our own judgments. We may not love the outfit she's wearing or the hairstyle she's chosen, but staying positive about her appearance helps her to see herself in a positive way. With the approach of puberty, girls need our support more than ever. But perhaps the most important part of that support has very little to do with what we say to our girls about their appearance at all; as their bodies begin to change, what they really need is to see us at peace with our own.

Making Peace with Your Own Body

Just as we're telling our girls that it's OK to leave behind the tiny little girl bodies of their childhoods and embrace the fuller bodies that puberty brings, we moms also have to leave behind the expectation that we *should* always look as we did when we were twenty-five. Rationally, we know this; in fact, I'm sure some of you are thinking, "Of course we can't look the way we did when we were twenty-five." Yet how many of us still lament the loss of our younger bodies, as if the process of getting older itself is something we could control if we just had the willpower?

Traci remembers her mom telling her not to have children in her thirties. "She told me the weight would never come off," she says. "She always told us that's when she got really heavy."

I've been guilty of making disparaging comments to Faith about my own post-baby body. After two C-sections, I've joked, I no longer have six-pack abs; instead, I've got a three-pack because my lower abs are buried under excess skin—a souvenir of pregnancy. I've been guilty of telling her that I'd never wear sweatpants with words across the backside because I'd need the large-print edition. Coming to terms with the changes in our bodies can be a tough process, especially when we hold ourselves to an idealized image from our past.

"I was really skinny as a child, and in my twenties I had a nice figure," forty-two-year-old Abby tells me. "When I had my kids, that's when I put it on. And because I always compared myself to my thinnest self, I thought I was so chubby. But I wasn't really chubby. It's a crazy thing to be a woman."

That was something I had to consider during my year writing the Weight-Loss Diary. When the editors asked me to set a goal weight, my immediate thought was 110 pounds; after all, that's what I weighed in high school, so why shouldn't I try to get back to it? Fortunately, I took a step back and realized that I'm twenty years older and have carried and given birth to two children. I might have been able to get down to 110 pounds, but at what price? Instead, I chose a goal weight of 125—my weight on my wedding day—a much more realistic and healthy weight for a forty-year-old mom of two.

It's Not Too Late to Change

Ideally, we'd all do nothing but send our daughters positive body messages from the time they're in the cradle. But what if you've been putting yourself down in front of your daughter for years? What if she's picked up on your bad behavior and has started to criticize her own body?

Fortunately, it's not too late to change the message you're sending. The good news is that you can talk to her about it. If she's open to it, ask her how she feels when you talk about your body that way. Or if she's following your example and putting herself down, tell her that you feel responsible for teaching her that behavior. Kids understand that adults make mistakes; in fact, it makes us seem more human to them.

"I don't think it's ever too late for parents to reverse some of the negative impact they may have had," says Dr. Vazzana. "But even more important than talking about it is showing them. Behavior matters as much as, if not more than, words."

Body Image Builders

Our daughters take their body image cues from us—not only the way we talk about *their* bodies, but the way we treat and talk about our own. Want to be a positive body image role model for your girl? Try these tactics:

Let her be her. OK, stripes with polka dots wouldn't be your first choice for an outfit, but if she loves it and feels good about the way she looks, try not to criticize. Many girls love to experiment with clothes and hair, and it's a great way for her to figure out who she is.

Don't do comedy. Humor can be a defense mechanism when you don't feel good about yourself, but your jokes about your body aren't fooling her. She gets the real message you're sending. It's OK to laugh together—even about your bodies, occasionally—but don't make your butt the "butt" of every joke.

Nix the "doom and gloom" comparisons. Avoid telling her that no matter what she does, she's destined to end up chubby like you or to have Great Aunt Edna's thighs. Even if you think it, don't say it.

Be her protector. If your mom or another relative makes critical comments to your daughter, step in and come to her defense. "Boy, you're getting chubby" can be buffered by "Are you kidding? She looks great." Make sure she knows you're on her side.

Should You Be Eating That?

Helping Your Daughter
Make Healthy Food Choices
(Without Making Her Feel Guilty)

> My favorite foods are fried chicken, chocolate,
> and cake. Sometimes my mom says, "I want you
> to be healthy," but usually she says, "Stop eating
> that chocolate!"
>
> —*Katherine, age fourteen*

Like many girls, I enjoyed a carefree childhood in
which cookies for a snack or a candy bar after
school were the norm. I was an active kid; gymnastics and ice skating built up powerful thigh muscles
that let me backflip my way across an open field and leave
the boys behind when we raced for team captain spots
during gym. My mom would roll her eyes and pretend we
weren't together as I cartwheeled my way down department store aisles. I spent afternoons running through a

string of neighborhood backyards with my friends; freeze tag, hide-and-seek, whiffle ball—we played them all with gusto for hours on end.

My body and how it looked simply weren't things I thought about. My mom would sometimes comment on my rounded, muscular thighs, but I didn't really worry about it. To me, they were a tool that let me run faster and flip higher. After-school snacks and nightly desserts fueled my adventures, and—at twelve years old—going up a clothing size wasn't cause for alarm. It just meant that I could finally shop in the juniors department.

One night, I reached for a cookie after dinner, and my mom said, "You know, you might want to cut back on the cookies."

It certainly wasn't the first time I'd been told I couldn't have a snack. But this felt different—what had been OK now wasn't. I had been OK, but now I wasn't.

In that single moment, I became a girl who had to worry about what she ate.

I think about that moment more and more now as I watch my own daughter. Does Faith notice me watching her scoop a second helping of mashed potatoes onto her plate? During a recent holiday gathering with our extended family, I watched my daughter reach out to take her third dinner roll, and I just couldn't stop myself. "Do you really need that roll?" I snapped. My twenty-four-year-old niece, who was sitting nearby, chided me: "What are you, the bun police?"

As I watched Faith's eyes fill with hurt, I realized that I'd done what I swore I'd never do.

I'd made her think she was that girl, too.

There wasn't one single thing that motivated my outburst that day. Maybe it was the relatives talking about how grown-up she looked. Maybe it was watching her walk away and recognizing my own shape in the curve of her hips. Maybe it was remembering her tearful struggle just days earlier in the department store dressing room when she couldn't find the "right" outfit. All I know is, in that moment, I didn't want her to ever feel the shame I had felt about my own body.

All moms see the best and worst of themselves in their daughters at times. And when you see a quality or behavior that reminds you of something in yourself that's caused you pain or shame, the urge to squelch it in her can feel overwhelming. Of all the body image issues that can arise between a mother and a daughter, food—and our relationship to it—is by far one of the most loaded. How many of us have spent a lifetime feeling that if we could just get control over the food we put in our mouths, we could control the way our bodies look? Or that if we could just get our daughters to cut back on the junk food, we could spare them the humiliation of being the "not quite right" girl we once were?

That sense of control is an illusion, of course, but that doesn't stop us from trying. Ever skipped dessert when you really wanted it, just had a salad, or frantically measured out food portions on a scale? Ever insisted that your daughter put back those cookies or told her she didn't need a second helping? Whether we focus on controlling the food we put in our own bodies or trying to control what our girls eat, we're teaching them that appetite is a beast that must be tamed.

Of course, it's not really that simple, either. Karin says she most wants to teach her daughter about self-control—and to not repeat her own bad habits—but Amanda resents her comments and suggestions.

"I can't really blame her for sitting down with a bag of chips," Karin says. "She's seen me do it, and she's seen my husband and boys do it. I get mad at myself because I know she's doing it because that's what I did. But I still have to be careful of how I say things because she does tend to get her feelings hurt. I just hope she realizes that I don't say any of this to hurt her."

It's our job as parents to teach our children healthy habits. But just how do you teach your daughter to eat healthfully without veering into unhealthy obsession—and doing more harm than good?

Eat by Example

Finding that line, without stepping over it, was one of my biggest concerns when I agreed to write the Weight-

Loss Diary. I knew that losing twenty-five pounds would demand a certain amount of food obsession, but I worried about Faith seeing me so fixated on what was going into my mouth—and what wasn't.

When I shared my concerns with Melissa, my dietitian for the project, she encouraged me to talk to Faith about not only what I was eating but the rationale behind it. Together, we learned about the value of lean protein in building muscle and boosting metabolism, about how being properly hydrated helps the body operate more efficiently, and how eating healthy, whole-grain carbohydrates immediately following a workout helps the body refuel after exertion.

Pretty technical stuff for a twelve-year-old, don't you think?

She may not adopt all of my new habits, but I'm hoping that the idea of eating for good health is sinking in and that Faith is filing that information away for future use in making her own decisions about food. After all, you can't force somebody to eat what they don't want to eat, at least not without consequences (let's just say I can remember wearing pureed peas a few times when Faith was a baby). But you can lead by example to show your daughter that having a healthy body—and even losing weight—doesn't require self-denial or starvation.

- **Emphasize health, not weight loss.** Frame your new eating habits within the science of good health, which takes the focus off simply eating less to lose weight (in fact, I ate more than I ever had). Try to casually incorporate the healthy changes you're making into the family's diet; don't force a new way of eating on her.

- **Walk the talk.** If we're talking to our daughters about the importance of putting nutritious food into their bodies as we're skipping lunch, we'd be fools to think that bit of hypocrisy will go unnoticed, even by the youngest of girls. Likewise, if I'm harping on my daughter to stop eating so much junk food as I'm feeding a nightly ice cream habit, my words aren't exactly credible, are they?

We're constantly sending our daughters messages about food and the role it plays in our lives, whether we mean to or not. Everything we do—from joyfully eating a piece of pizza to ordering a salad instead of a baked potato to complaining to a friend about the dessert we shouldn't have eaten—sends our girls a message.

Abby, now forty-two, remembers going on her first date and being horrified when the boy wanted to order pizza. "I remember thinking, 'Eat pizza in front of a boy? What? I can't eat pizza in front of a boy,'" she tells me. "My mom never ate 'fattening' stuff. She never ate anything sweet. There was almost an attitude of 'Girls aren't supposed to eat that.' She definitely deprived herself."

Rather than deprivation, Abby—who has struggled with her own weight and recently lost thirty pounds—

tries to make it easy for her fifteen-year-old daughter, Tammy, to eat a healthy diet. She stocks her house with food items like cooked chicken, salad fixings, whole-wheat bread, and other nutritious choices. And she makes sure that Tammy sees her eating.

In spite of eating healthfully, though, Abby says her daughter is the largest of her group of friends and that she always feels heavy and worries about being too big. "She's a beautiful girl," she tells me. "But she's a big-boned girl, and she's heavier than she looks. She has big hands and feet, and she's tall like a model. But in high school, you don't look at it that way. Her best friend is this tiny little thing."

Though nature may have given Tammy her large bone structure, Abby believes in the importance of nurture and absolutely considers herself a role model for her daughter. She tries to set a positive tone when it comes to eating and to show Tammy that it's OK to treat yourself. "I make sure I get healthy snacks like sugar-free Jell-O and Popsicles, just to show her that you can snack, [but] you just have to make good choices," she says. "And it did teach her that you don't need to eat the junk."

Still, Abby's voice is wistful when she talks about how having to watch what she eats affects Tammy's life. Everything her friends do seems to revolve around food, she says, and most of Tammy's friends are small girls who seem to be able to eat whatever they want. That's tough for both mother and daughter to watch, but Abby says she's trying to teach Tammy to trust herself to make her own choices.

"She went out to dinner with her friends one time, and she texted me and said, 'What should I order?'" Abby tells me. "And I felt so sad, you know? I was thinking, 'Order some french fries and a sundae. You're out with your friends. You're beautiful.'"

Mothers play a powerful role in shaping their daughters' relationship with food. That's why modeling healthy eating habits instead of just talking about them—eating a good mix of healthy foods, enjoying treats in moderation, and trusting your own body to tell you when it's hungry—is one of the most positive things you can do for your daughter.

Giving Up Control

For a lot of us, wanting to keep our daughters from feeling the shame we've felt about our bodies drives us to comment on and critique their dietary choices—as I did to Faith during the dinner roll incident. But a heavy-handed approach to trying to control her eating can really backfire. For a girl who's truly struggling with how she feels about her body, too much emphasis on calories and pounds does nothing but cause hurt feelings that last forever.

At thirty-seven, Cindy can't remember a time when watching her weight wasn't part of her life. "My mom was a heavy kid, and that was very scarring to her," she says. Her mom constantly monitored what she ate, she says, starting when she was about seven years old.

As a result, she and her sister, Nancy, age forty-one, would often sneak food when their mom wasn't around. That intense focus on calories and pounds during her childhood led Cindy to eat whatever she wanted when she was finally out on her own. "I was no longer living under her roof," she says. "It became, 'I can eat what I want. No one's here to tell me I can't go to the grocery store and buy what I want.' So I did." As a result, she says, her weight quickly ballooned.

Nancy says that even though she wasn't a chubby kid, that didn't stop her mother from making comments about what she was eating. "If I came home from school and went to get a snack, [Mom would] say, 'What are you doing? You're going to get fat. Why are you eating that?'" she says, adding that she still struggles to understand her mom's behavior when she looks at pictures of herself as a skinny child.

Now Cindy and Nancy are determined that the girls in their family won't pack on the pounds the way they did and spend a lifetime obsessed with their weight.

Indeed, we moms have to be especially careful about criticizing eating habits we helped to create. Often, says Dr. Laura Jana, pediatrician and coauthor of *Food Fights*, moms encourage their young children to eat more because they're concerned by the normal slowdown in children's appetites between the ages of one and eight. Then these same moms start to panic when growth (and appetite) picks up again near puberty, and they criticize their girls for simply doing what they were taught to do. But that's not really fair, is it? No wonder our girls end up feeling hurt, angry, and confused.

Twelve-year-old Kristen says her mom is constantly telling her that she needs to eat healthier foods and exercise more. "I hate it when she says I need to eat better," she tells me. "She talks about it way too much."

Amanda, age thirteen, says that although her mom often tells her to cut down on what she's eating, the real pressure comes from her grandmother. "She constantly tells me I need to lose weight and then lectures me," she says. "It's so stressful!"

To Talk or Not to Talk about Food?

If your mom criticized your eating habits or fixated constantly on your weight, you may not want to bring the topic up at all with your own daughter for fear of making her feel bad about herself. I felt so awful after the dinner roll incident with Faith that I went out of my way *not* to comment on what or how much she was eating—even if I secretly worried that it was too much.

When it comes to talking about food choices—especially as they relate to weight—it's best to take your cues directly from your daughter. If she's healthy and generally makes good choices, there's really no need to step in with "preventative" talk of calories and fat grams and weight gain. But what if your daughter has witnessed your own struggles with weight and food? What should you say to help her understand that your struggles are about your body feelings, not hers?

It's OK to talk about those struggles, but do it during a moment when emotions aren't running high, says Dr. Jana. In general, it's not as effective to simply make "You don't want to end up like me" comments. "A better approach is to talk about how much more we know now about healthy eating and its effect on our bodies than when you were younger—and that you're glad she'll be able to grow up and make her own healthy choices about what's right for her," she says.

Serve Up a Healthy Conversation

Let your daughter know that eating a variety of healthful foods is the best way to keep her body healthy, strong, and looking good.

This is an area where the much-maligned media can actually be beneficial; everything from advertisements for hundred-calorie snack items to photographs of skin-and-bones celebrities can serve as conversation starters about healthy eating. By using these images as a springboard, you can talk to her about how important it is to eat a healthy diet without making it about *her* diet. That's how you avoid "My mom thinks I'm fat, so she's talking to me about food" scenarios.

Tread carefully.

Know, too, that fluctuating hormones and a new pre-occupation with adolescent concerns means that girls at this age are rarely logical. If you're going to talk about food and food choices, you'll need to tread carefully. A well-meaning comment—"Wow, you're really enjoying that pizza"—can easily be taken as a criticism, and the hurt from a "good-natured" joke about her appetite can last for years.

Limit conversation about food—especially as it relates to weight.

Sometimes, the best thing you can do is to remove your-self from the equation. Maura, age thirty-seven, started dieting at age ten, but says she's taking a different ap-proach with her daughters, who are nine and twelve. Each night, Maura—who says she spent all of her pre-teen years, her adolescence, and her twenties feeling bad about the way she looked—serves a healthy meal of lean protein, green vegetables, and potato or pasta. Her girls are allowed to take what they want, leave what they want, and finish—or not finish—their food as they see fit, but they don't talk about it. Because of that, Maura says, they're both excellent eaters who'll try new foods.

"Because of all the baggage I carry from my childhood, I'm very conscious of the way I talk about exercise, food, and weight," she tells me. "I like to cook, so I cook healthy meals. I just don't make a big deal out of it. My mom used to make special meals for my younger sister. It was like a three-ring circus at dinnertime. And God forbid you didn't finish something that was on your plate."

Involve your daughter in preparing meals.

Letting our girls take the lead in what and how much they eat is a valuable first step in teaching them to listen to their own bodies. But while she's learning to listen to her body's cues about hunger, she continues to look to you as an example. If she's interested, this is a great time to involve your daughter in meal preparation; one of Faith's favorite things to do is make fruit salad for the family. When our daughters join us in the kitchen, not only do they absorb valuable information about healthy eating, they also enjoy spending time with us—something girls often crave in early adolescence but may not know how to ask for.

Relaxed opportunities to hang out together in the kitchen are also a terrific time to get a sense of what's on her mind. If she's suddenly interested in the calorie counts of the foods you're preparing or if she's talking about a friend who thinks she's fat, consider that your cue to safely broach the topic of eating habits.

When Your Daughter Has a Weight Problem

But suppose your daughter really does have a weight problem that's growing because of her poor eating habits? Those are tricky waters, but you can navigate your way through. Above all, resist the urge to point out that she's getting overweight. Trust me, if she's got a weight problem, she already knows—you don't have to say a word. When it comes to addressing serious weight problems, make a family commitment to healthy eating. The worst thing you can do is single her out.

That's what forty-eight-year-old Carolyn tries to keep in mind. Her twelve-year-old daughter, Kristen, has put on quite a bit of weight during puberty, but Carolyn is taking what she calls a "global" approach to dealing with Kristen's weight problem. She preaches moderation and offers Kristen choices: Hot cocoa *or* cake? Chips *or* cookies? Kristen loves fettuccine Alfredo, so Carolyn makes it at home, where she can control the ingredients used.

Is that approach working? Carolyn's not sure, but she's committed to staying the course. "I don't really say anything because I think when you're ready to lose weight, you will," she says. "I do try to make it her responsibility and her choice. She's a bit of a difficult personality, and I can see where things I say to her will affect her for a long time."

That's for sure. As moms, when we focus on diets and calories and weight, we're planting the seed that it's not OK to gain weight—a dangerous concept at puberty, when some weight gain is absolutely appropriate and necessary for our girls and their health. Melissa, my *Shape* dietitian, goes so far as to say moms should *never* tell kids they're overweight or even use the word "diet" in front of them.

As for your daughter's eating habits, are you filling your cupboards with junk food and asking her not to eat it? Serving quick, not-so-healthy meals because of time and schedule constraints?

Karin, age forty-eight, knows all too well about the impact she's had on her girl when it comes to eating. Her daughter, Amanda, now weighs more than she does, and Karin blames herself for that. "The doctor's been very frank," she tells me. "He asked me, 'Who does the grocery shopping?' and all of a sudden it clicked: if I don't bring home chips and ice cream, they're not going to eat it."

Talking to our girls about healthy eating is so tricky because food remains such a loaded topic for so many of us, even as adults. When I was writing the Weight-Loss Diary, the question I was most often asked was: "What are you eating?" Likewise, when I write about food in my blog, those entries always generate the most reader comments. And think about all the ways we pass along our own biases about food to our girls; at a friend's party recently I had a conversation with an eight-year-old who told me that her much-older babysitter calls Oreo cookies "fat pills." When I asked her why she called them that, she looked at me as if I were an idiot and said, "Because they make you fat if you eat them."

I don't know about you, but I don't want my daughter to grow up thinking she can't treat herself to a cookie without fear of getting fat. That's why it's just as important for our girls to see us indulge from time to time as it is for them to see us eating our vegetables. Letting go of the need to micromanage every bite that goes into our mouths—and theirs—is the only way to show our daughters that food is for nourishment and enjoyment, and that there's room for both in life.

Body Image Builders

Food can be a loaded topic between moms and their daughters, but you can set her on the path to healthy eating without making her feel guilty or implying that she needs to change. Here's what to do and say—and what not to say—when it comes to food:

Don't criticize. We all make occasional bad choices. If you see her sitting on the couch with an entire bag of chips, mindlessly munching, employ a parenting tactic from the toddler years: Redirect. Ask her if she'd like to go for a walk or if she'd like a cup of cocoa. Then gently try to draw out what might be bothering her. Is she bored? Stressed about a test? Upset about a fight with a friend? Sometimes mindless snacking is about so much more than a craving for chips.

Strategize at the store. Take a look in your cart, and make sure you're gathering what you need to show her what balanced eating looks like. Aim for a mix of fruits, vegetables, proteins, whole grains, and, yes, treats.

Watch out for hidden messages. Think buying only low-fat, fat-free, and sugar-free items is a surefire path to healthy eating? Not necessarily. Remember, a fridge full of only fat-free choices sends a message. Make sure it's one you want to send.

Make her a partner. If your daughter expresses an interest in healthy eating, have her help you plan meals and make grocery lists. Ask her what healthy snacks she'd like for lunches or for after school. But don't force the issue; let her dictate how involved she wants to be.

Time your talks. If you do decide to bring up your daughter's eating habits with her, don't do it when either of you is upset—and don't use information she's shared with you against her. Avoid comments like, "You say you're getting fat, but look, you're eating a bowl of ice cream."

Mom's Got Game

Helping Our Girls Learn to Love Fitness (Without Focusing on Fat)

> Do you count marching band as a sport? I definitely do, and that's my regular exercise. It's more physically demanding than most people think.
>
> —*Amanda, age thirteen*

It's the bottom of the fourth inning in Faith's Little League fast-pitch softball game, and she's on the pitcher's mound. It's been a rough game; I can see her frustration in the way she pinches her lips together just before she throws the ball. She's walked the last few batters, and she's losing heart. She glances at the coach and at her dad on the sidelines. "Take me out," her eyes are saying. "I don't think I can do this."

But the coach doesn't make a move. So she takes a deep breath, winds up, and lets the ball fly.

"Strike," calls the umpire.

Her smile spreads from ear to ear, and I want to leap out of my seat and scream. But like any self-respecting thirteen-year-old, she'd be mortified if I did that, so I clap politely instead and yell, "Good job, honey."

This is what sports is all about.

I love that she's found a passion that tests her mental and physical limits. I love that she's learning to keep going when she thinks she can't. And I love that absolutely none of it has anything to do with the way her body looks.

It's exactly what I *didn't* experience as a kid.

I was four years old when Title IX (the 1972 federal law requiring gender equity in school sports) was passed, and there weren't a ton of options for girls to play team sports when I was growing up. For me, organized physical activities beyond gym class were mostly about dance and cheerleading, both of which required a certain athletic ability, but the focus wasn't on winning games (at least, not as a player). Back then, in cheerleading at my school, it was mainly on looking cute and showing off your budding sex appeal (although we certainly considered ourselves athletes and took home honors in several cheerleading competitions). In dance, the focus was on using your body as an instrument of expression—and the more beautiful your instrument, the greater your success.

There's nothing wrong with looking cute or beautiful, of course, and today's cheerleaders are way more athletic than we ever were. But in those sports where appearance is a big part of what determines "success," the competitive aspect can become a lot different from the kind of competition team sports encourage; it's a pressure to look perfect that I'm not sure basketball or soccer players feel. To this day, I can recall the exact moment when I learned that the bigger body puberty had brought me was now a liability in my sport.

I was an acrobat through most of my childhood—a good one, in fact. I competed in some tough competitions, and one of the toughest used to offer teachers cassette tapes they could listen to after the performances. During a dancer's routine, the judges would talk into a tape recorder and comment on what they were seeing—sort of like an early *American Idol* for dancers.

When I was fourteen, I took third place in the solo acrobatic category, quite a respectable finish. I went to the studio for my lesson the following week, eager to hear what the judges said about my routine. My teacher played my tape, and together we listened as the judges offered helpful feedback on my timing, technical execution, and overall presentation. But as the song came to an end, a male judge said loudly into the microphone, "This performer could really stand to drop a few pounds."

It was like being slapped in the face. Suddenly, I was ashamed—and furious that a criticism of my body had been the final word on a good performance. I dropped out of acrobatics shortly after that, tired of the pressure to look perfect in costumes made for girls much tinier than I now was. I might have been an excellent acrobat, but I no longer looked the part.

My mom didn't say much about my quitting, but she did say, "You need to keep moving." The message was loud and clear: If you don't do something, you'll end up fat. Physical activity wasn't her thing; the most exercise I saw her get was walking from her car into the store to buy cigarettes. But she was determined that I would stay active. Getting too big simply wasn't going to be an option for me.

By high school, I'd dropped more than thirty pounds, courtesy of an eating disorder, and made the cheerleading squad. She couldn't have been more proud; in her day, cheerleading was a one-way ticket to high school popularity. But part of me longed to be the one excelling on the field, rather than cheering from the sidelines. I envied the girls who ran track or played basketball.

Getting Them Moving

Chances are, you may be witnessing the double-edged sword of adolescence with your own daughter: Just as our girls put on the normal weight that comes with puberty, many of them are also becoming less active, whether it's because of time constraints, put-downs, or a general lack of motivation. That can lead to more weight gain and even less activity, setting off a downward spiral of feeling bad about their bodies. According to a 2007 research re-

port on developing physically active girls by the Tucker
Center for Research on Women and Girls in Sport at
the University of Minnesota, not only do girls perceive
physical activity as less important than boys do, they're
also less motivated and feel less competent.[1]

Why is that? There are a couple of factors at play, says
Lynda Ransdell, PhD, professor and chair of the Department of Kinesiology at Boise State University, who has
studied what happens when mothers and daughters exercise together. First, there are many different things competing for girls' time. "Voice mail, email, computer games,
and instant messaging are sometimes more interesting
to girls at this age," she tells me. "But adolescents are also
really self-conscious; their bodies are changing, and they're
very hesitant to do anything that's outside of the norm."

What can you do if your daughter shows no interest
in sports whatsoever or hates being active? That can be
challenging, but you can show your girl that being active doesn't have to involve running or competing or
even copious amounts of sweat. And sometimes the
promise of time spent alone with Mom can be a great
motivator to step away from the computer. I can almost
always talk Faith into taking a walk with me; not only
are we both getting exercise, but we're also getting some
uninterrupted time to talk and stay connected.

A simple walk in the evening, a hike through the
woods on the weekend, or a teen program at a local
YMCA might be just appealing enough to get her off

the couch. But if it's not, some moms, like Carolyn, try to "sneak" exercise into their daughters' lives.

"My youngest really hates to exercise because she's overweight," she tells me. "But I have her walk home from school, and that's about a mile. I've also made it her chore to walk the dog every day. I think encouraging exercise is important because when you do something physical, you just always feel better about your body."

For forty-nine-year-old Rachel, a former dancer, exercise is all about the movement itself. She teaches movement classes, swims, and does yoga, and she and her husband often rollerblade together and ride bikes. "You'll rarely find me weight lifting or doing something for the sake of making something better," she tells me. "I never think of it as 'I've got to go work out.'"

Her three daughters, ages nineteen, seventeen, and fourteen, have all been active in sports at one point or another and continue to be occasionally, but none of them is what Rachel would call a fitness enthusiast—a fact that sometimes frustrates her.

"They're big readers and hang-arounders," she says. "And it's really interesting to me because we're so active and they're just—not. I try hard not to make them wrong, but I want them to be healthy."

Encourage your daughter to try a sport.

Remember Abby, who tried to set a good healthy eating example for her fifteen-year-old daughter, Tammy? She's encouraged Tammy to find a sport she loves, too. Abby was an all-American swimmer in college herself and is thrilled that Tammy has discovered lacrosse and also likes to swim. Being active in sports has been great not only for Tammy's fitness level, Abby tells me, but for her self-image.

"Her happiest, most balanced time is when she's involved in some type of athletics," she says. "She's putting on a bathing suit and going swimming—when else are you going to have body issues? But she appreciates the fact that she's in shape and she's doing well, and it kind of helps her see past the whole picking on every bulge and bump. She sees that she's strong and athletic."

According to the Women's Sports Foundation, girls and women who play sports have a more positive body image and more confidence and bring more teamwork and goal-setting skills into the workplace.[2] Sports and exercise also help girls reduce their risk of some future health problems, like breast cancer and osteoporosis. But while sports offer plenty of benefits to a girl who plays, whether she ever starts depends very much on the message she gets at home.

When she was little, Faith tried a bunch of different activities—dance classes, gymnastics, and soccer—before she decided that softball was it for her. Encouraging your daughter to try new things and not insisting that she stick with something long term that she clearly doesn't enjoy mean she'll be able to find that sport she wants to do, just for the love of it.

Focus on athletic achievement, not athletic (or physical) perfection.

Although I didn't always appreciate the message behind it, looking back, I'm grateful that my mom pushed me to stay physically active as a teenager. Somewhere along the way, I rediscovered the joy of moving my body, and it's a joy that's stayed with me into adulthood. In my thirties, I even gave team sports a try when I played in an over-thirty women's recreational soccer league. I was an awful player; I didn't know the rules of the game, I thought for sure I'd collapse and die from all that running back and forth, and, frankly, some of those "recreational" players were a bit too competitive. I took more than a few elbows in the corner while fighting for the ball. One night, I got slammed into the wall so hard that I remember thinking, "Why am I doing this? I'm somebody's mother."

I was doing it to show myself—and my daughter—that staying active isn't about having the "perfect" body. Some of those players were much heavier than I was, but that didn't stop them from playing their hardest. Finding a sport you love—though, alas, soccer wasn't it for me—can lead to a lifelong friendship with exercise and, to some degree, with your body. We may not always love the way our bodies look, but there's a certain appreciation that comes with giving your best physical effort, no matter what it is. Whether it's the thrill of running a 5K, the sweaty glow from a good dance class, the tight muscles from a strength-training session, or even the good kind of tired that comes from a day of working in the garden, it's hard to hate your body when it's just met a tough challenge.

Make it about enjoying movement and gaining skills, not losing pounds.

Lisa, age forty-two and the mother of ten-year-old Laurie, says she learned a lot from watching her mom, who was a lifelong tennis player. "I played tennis, and I was encouraged to play because both of my parents played," she tells me. "It was just a natural part of our lives. I still play, and I like that Laurie sees that. I also tell her that it really makes me happy to be active and that if I'm happy, everyone at home is usually happy."

In our family, we try to live by a simple rule: Everybody has to have a physical activity that he or she enjoys, and we all have to do it regularly. It's not about weight loss—it's about doing something you love, just for the fun of it, and keeping your body healthy in the process.

Like Mother, Like Daughter

Early adolescence is clearly a turning point when it comes to laying the foundation for a lifetime of healthy exercise habits. But we can't simply order our daughters off the couch and onto the field. We can tell them how important it is to be active, but if we do it from our own perch on the couch, they'll just tune us out. If we want them to sweat a bit, we've got to be willing to sweat a bit, too.

"My mom is constantly on the move," says Sophie, fifteen. "Either she's taking a yoga class, swimming in a mini-triathlon, teaching a hydrofit class, or just taking a ride on her bike. She usually asks me to come along, and sometimes I do."

Setting an example for your daughter is a great way to encourage her to get moving. You don't have to be the most talented athlete in the world to be a positive role model.

Pam, forty-five-year-old mom to twelve-year-old Allison, didn't feel athletic enough to join any teams back in high school. "I played softball, but I was the worst player for five years running," she tells me. But she doesn't let her perceived lack of athletic prowess stop her from showing Allison that it's good to try something new. "I entered a 5K race three years ago and came in dead last. But I did finish—behind the guy picking up the cones."

Our daughters can learn a lot from seeing us try something new and stick with it, even if it's tough. Cutting ourselves some slack and eliminating our need to be perfect at everything we try go a long way toward showing them that exercise can be fun and doesn't have to be this serious, goal-oriented activity. Pam's attitude of "Hey, I didn't win, but I tried my best" is such a healthy one. When we're willing to step outside of our own comfort zone and risk having people find out—*horrors!*—that we're not perfect, we show our daughters that living a healthy life and loving our bodies enough to take care of them can be fun. A willingness to experiment and to look foolish while doing it is something many girls lose in adolescence and early adulthood.

Dealing with the Pressure

As with healthy eating, we've got to be careful that, whether through our words or our own example, we don't make being physically active simply about losing pounds. That was one of the things that most terrified me during my year as *Shape*'s Weight-Loss Diary columnist, but I felt powerless to stop it. Suddenly, moving my body was no longer about staying active for the fun of it, and Faith definitely picked up on the change in my attitude. Gone were the walks I used to take down to the beach just to watch the sun set and the adult hip-hop dance class where we spent half our time dancing and the other half giggling about how we couldn't master the moves. Now, my extra time was spent Going To The Gym.

In the pressure-cooker experience of being photographed monthly for a magazine—and knowing that the editors and readers were expecting to *see* progress—exercise became all about getting smaller. I spent hours on the treadmill and elliptical trainer, staring mindlessly at the "calories burned" number that appeared on the screen, while sunny skies and warm breezes waited just outside the gym door. I pushed myself harder and harder, until my knees burned, my hips ached, and my back throbbed.

"Are you OK, Mom?" Faith asked me one night as I sat with the heating pad on my back and an ice pack on my knee.

"I'm just sore from the gym," I told her.

She looked at me curiously, as if she was wondering why I was doing this to myself.

Why, indeed?

Don't get me wrong; I love exercise and the way my body feels after a good workout—the endorphin high, the muscles a little sore. But during my year with *Shape*, exercise went from being something I enjoyed to an obligation that was all about an end goal. In my zeal to see results, I pushed myself harder and harder and harder. I don't mean to imply that exercise isn't work; it certainly is, though if you're lucky enough to find an activity you love, it often doesn't feel that way. And sometimes exercise feels like an obligation. But to me, there's a difference between feeling obligated to move your body to keep it as healthy as it can be and the soul-numbing obsession with "working out" simply to watch the number on the scale get lower and lower.

When my column with *Shape* ended, I found myself going to the gym less and less. It wasn't that I didn't want to stay active—I was just burned out from trying to attain a more "perfect" version of myself. So I started taking walks again. I took a dance class. I went ice skating. And I remembered how much I like to exercise, just for the way it makes my body feel. Now I occasionally head to the gym when the weather is lousy, but mostly do strength-training workouts at home and walk for cardio. Working out on my own terms feels good again, without all that pressure.

Faith knows a little bit about feeling pressured to perform. Though she's very fit, she doesn't like to run for long periods of time—so much so that she refuses to play soccer, even though all her friends do. A former gym teacher would start each class with a one-mile run, and Faith often came in at the back of the pack. The teacher would tell the kids, "This is what separates the fit from the unfit," leaving Faith feeling judged—and furious.

Many girls (and adult women) struggle with the idea that they need to wait until they've lost weight or look better in workout clothes or are able to do an activity perfectly before they'll do it. Let's face it, plodding your way through a dance or aerobics class where everyone else seems to already know the steps or facing a gym full of equipment that you're not sure how to use is intimidating.

Maura didn't like to play sports because she had trouble getting past her need to be perfect. "I would always try things, but if I wasn't good at them right away, I wouldn't want to do it," she says. "I once tried to play basketball, but I didn't get it in the first fifteen minutes, so I thought, 'Well, I'm not good at basketball.'"

Judgment—and the pressure to perform or excel—is another place where we have to be careful about the messages we send to our daughters, says Dr. Ransdell, especially at this sensitive time in their lives. "It can be a very fine line," she acknowledges. "But the better message is that it's all about having fun and staying strong."

After the gym class incident, Faith and I talked about how moving your body doesn't have to be about reaching a goal weight or about somebody else's vision of a good finish. During my year with *Shape*, she got to witness firsthand what gym obsession looks like. It isn't pretty. Now that it's over, she's seen me rediscover a much more balanced approach to exercise. But something good and unexpected did come out of the gym obsession I experienced. Being pushed to my limits by a personal trainer forced me to let go of my need to be perfect and required a willingness to try things I'd never tried before. That's a great message for any mom to send to her daughter.

Body Image Builders

Moms willing to sweat often have daughters who are willing to sweat, too. Finding a physical activity or sport that you love to do encourages her to find one that she loves. Want to see your girl get moving and love it? Keep this advice in mind:

Praise effort, not performance. If she's involved in a competitive sport, keep the focus on giving her best effort, not on the scoreboard's final outcome.

Practice, don't preach. Before you tell her to play outside, go ride her bike, or do something physical, know that she may think you're criticizing her body. Try saying, "Hey, want to go take a walk with me? I need some fresh air."

Arrange for instruction. Fear of looking foolish is a big hindrance to being active for a lot of girls. If there's a sport she's always wanted to try, but she's afraid she'll look silly, consider paying for a private lesson or two to help her learn the basics.

Keep it fun. Exercise doesn't always have to be serious business. Challenge her to a jump rope contest, a backyard kickball game, or a living room dance-off.

Offer logistical support. A huge part of getting and keeping girls active in sports is making sure they have the support they need, whether it's a ride to practice, a cheering fan in the stands, or the right equipment. Make sure your daughter knows she can count on you to support her efforts.

PART 2

Measuring Up

Am I More if I'm Less?

Getting Past the Numbers Game

> It seems like most girls think they're fat.
>
> —*Michaela, age twelve*

I f working out is the one thing that can usually be counted on to make us feel good about our bodies, stepping on the scale is the one thing that can usually be counted on to make us feel bad—unless, of course, the numbers are in our favor. It's amazing how much power we give to a silly little measurement.

And it *is* silly.

When I signed on to write the Weight-Loss Diary, I most dreaded stepping on that scale each month for an "official" weigh-in that would then be reported to *millions* of readers. Not only did I dread people knowing what I weighed, I dreaded stepping back into that cycle of living by a number. See, I was a bit of a scale-obsessed teen; it began the day I dragged our dust-covered analog version out from under the bathroom sink, where it hadn't seen the light of day in years. When it came to the scale, my own mother's message was crystal clear: If you don't know the number, it can't hurt you. This was a woman who'd only agree to be weighed at the doctor's office if the nurse promised not to tell her what the number was.

My approach as a young teenager was radically different. I'd hop on that scale every single morning—and sometimes at night, too—and adjust my mood based on what it said. A pound down buoyed my confidence so much that I'd easily smile at the cutest guy in school, while a pound up meant hiding behind turtlenecks, long sweaters, and hair hanging down into my face. It was a game that continued even through college (I used a friend's scale) and beyond, until I got married and left the scale behind at my childhood home.

Living without that metallic master—and without the daily up-and-down, gripping fear of encroaching pounds—was a freedom I'd long forgotten. But two pregnancies and the comfort of marriage brought on the pounds that I'd long worked to keep away. When I went in for a physical at the age of thirty-five, I was shocked when the nurse told me my weight: 155 pounds.

It was the most I'd *ever* weighed without a baby growing in my belly.

By the time the *Shape* column came my way, I was back down to 147 pounds (I'd stopped swallowing my grief over my mom's death with chocolate at that point). On the day that I was officially weighed for my first column, I went home and cried, ashamed not only of how I'd "let myself go," but also of the fact that everyone I knew would see that number in print. I was also terrified by the expectation that the number would drop each month. The pressure felt as enormous as I did!

Early on, I decided not to buy a scale to use at home because I knew I wouldn't be able to fight the temptation to step on it every day. I didn't want my day's eating and activities—or my mood—to be colored by what it said. Mostly, though, I didn't want to introduce Faith to the idea that stepping on the scale was a way to measure her self-worth. For her, I wanted weight to be simply another innocent measurement taken at the doctor's office each year.

But since the whole point of the Weight-Loss Diary column is, in fact, to lose weight, I knew there was no avoiding the scale and its power over me. So Faith and I had a long talk—one of many—about weighing yourself and the importance of "pounds." We talked about body composition, including bone structure, blood volume, and muscle mass, and we talked about how a person's weight is just one part of her overall health picture. We talked about how a very fit person can be heavier than an unfit person, and how people who may seem ideal if you were to consider just their weight might not be so healthy after all. We also talked about things that can affect the number on the scale: Am I drinking enough water? Did I eat a salty meal recently? (I learned about that factor the hard way when I ate Chinese food the night before one of my weigh-ins for the magazine.) What time of the month is it? Did I use the bathroom recently? All these things can make the number swing as much as four or five pounds—something I never knew before I started writing the column and certainly evidence of how silly a measurement weight can actually be.

Of course, Faith was very interested in the results of each weigh-in. She was thrilled for me when I'd lost a pound or two, so thrilled in fact that it gave me a bit of a sick feeling inside. "This isn't right," I remember thinking. "This is a bad seed to be planting." But she was also on hand for the months when I didn't lose any weight at all, even though I'd been eating according to my plan and working out like a fiend. That's when we'd have yet another talk about keeping "the number" in perspective. The needle may not have moved, but I'd increased my muscle mass and decreased my body fat percentage, and I had more energy than I'd had in years. Always, I tried to point out how much healthier I was becoming.

Still, it was hard not to feel judged as a failure when I hadn't lost any weight or body fat. One particular month, when I'd already lost nineteen pounds and dropped three sizes, my official testing revealed that my body fat number had crept up by .8 percent. When I reported that number to my editors, they seemed shocked. "What happened?" they asked.

Nothing happened.

I'd been diligent about eating and exercise, and yet I couldn't force that number to go down. When I told Faith about the incident, including my editors' semi-accusatory tone, she smiled and rolled her eyes in typical preteen "whatever" fashion, and suddenly I felt victorious. She grasped the absurdity of the whole thing.

Judged by the Pound

Just because she got it, however, doesn't mean Faith is immune to the lure of the scale. Recently, the school nurse completed height and weight measurements during gym class. Although it was done privately, girls were comparing their stats afterward. When she came home from school that day, she told me her weight and also shared the weights that some of her friends had reported.

"Is that OK?" she asked me after revealing her number.

"That's perfect," I told her.

And it *was* perfect. She's a growing girl whose body is changing.

Given how quickly their bodies are changing, it's no wonder that many adolescents are constantly scrutinizing themselves and monitoring how they measure up to their peers, whether it's through the number on the scale or the number on the label inside their jeans— and it isn't only girls who worry that they might be too heavy.

Fifteen-year-old Sophie has a history of digestive problems that make it hard for her to gain weight. "Generally, I wear a size 0, and right now I weigh about 90 pounds," she says. "It's really hard for me to gain weight. I hate people talking about their weight and how fat they feel and how they wish they had my body. . . . It's funny, actually, because I've been on the other side, wishing I actually did weigh 120 pounds."

As girls grow and mature, fluctuations in body weight and in height are common. They may gain more weight one year, but then shoot up the next. Growth of any kind rarely follows a straight path—it's always full of twists and turns—but how we respond to that growth makes a difference in whether our daughters see themselves as "normal" or as having some sort of problem.

During her most recent physical, the nurse completed Faith's height and weight measurements, and then marked them on her chart. I waited until Faith stepped out of the room to use the bathroom before I asked the nurse what her weight was and how it compared to last year's. I was thrilled to hear that she's growing normally and in a healthy way. She came back, and a few minutes later, the doctor came in, grabbed Faith's chart, and said breezily, "Your height and weight have evened out. That's great because last year you were a little bit chunky. Are you doing something differently?"

Chunky?!

I glanced over at Faith and saw a wave of panic wash over her face. "Chunky" is not a word that anyone would have used to describe her, last year or now. I was so shocked by the doctor's use of that word that all I could do was blurt out, "She's eating healthy foods and playing softball, just like always." Later, as I thought about it, I got angrier and angrier. Why would any doctor, knowing how sensitive adolescent girls can be about their bodies, choose to use that word when talking with a patient?

Michelle May, MD, a family physician and author of *Am I Hungry? What to Do When Diets Don't Work*, doesn't agree with the doctor's word choice, but does understand where the doctor was coming from. According to her, doctors today are being bombarded with messages about childhood obesity and are therefore more likely to bring up the subject of weight with their patients, even with those who don't have a weight problem. Teaching kids about the importance of maintaining a healthy weight is a good thing, of course. But we all—mothers, teachers, friends, and even doctors—have to be careful of what we say about weight to our girls. "Although she doesn't have a weight problem, what [Faith] probably heard was, 'I was chunky, I could be again, and somebody noticed,'" says Dr. May.

Of course, it isn't just our feelings about our own weight that help shape how we feel about our bodies. It's what other people say about *their* weight, too. A few years ago, my husband and I attended a dinner party at the home of another couple we know. After dinner, the men moved into the living room, while the women sat around the table talking. The subject soon turned to weight, and as the women began to reveal their weights, each prefaced or followed by a comment about how "fat" they were, I soon realized that I was the heaviest woman at the table. If I hadn't been feeling bad about my body before that incident, you can bet I was feeling bad about it then.

It's like that for our daughters, too. When kids are young, they're rarely thinking about how much they weigh or how they can maintain their weight. Over time, though, there's a subtle shift as they start to tune in to what their moms, grandmas, and other adult women are talking about. When they see us so concerned by the number on the scale, they also start to be concerned. But remember, in early adolescence, our girls are putting on the necessary pounds their bodies need to change into women. If we teach them that seeing the number on the scale rise is cause for self-hatred, how can we expect them to be at peace with their maturing bodies?

Remember Karin, whose thirteen-year-old daughter Amanda is now bigger than she is? She remembers telling Amanda about how envious she always was of her sister because she wore a size smaller than Karin did when they were growing up. "I said, 'She was always skinnier than me. And that was when I weighed 140,'" she says. "And Amanda said, 'Well, I'm really envious of you, Mom, because I'll never weigh 140.' That was really hard."

Our girls need our reassurance that the weight they're gaining at this point in their lives is both normal and OK with us. The best way to offer that reassurance is to not make a big deal about the number at all.

"I've had girls step on the scale and Mom would be peering over their shoulder, saying, 'Wow, you've gained a lot of weight,'" says Dr. May. "When we talk about how 'good' we look, label certain foods 'good' or 'bad,' or worry about the scale, we're teaching them that weight is an area they have to focus on. We teach them to think we might be measuring them and assessing their value based on the scale or on a clothing size."

You Look Great. Did You Lose Weight?

If we feel happy when we look in the mirror, what does it matter what a metal box tells us? And yet so many of us give so much importance to that number and to the very idea of losing weight. Have you ever run into an old friend who says, "You look great. Have you lost weight?" It's considered a high compliment. Most of us respond with comments like, "Really? Thanks" or "I'm trying" or even my standard smart-alecky "You're my new best friend."

But have you ever stopped and thought about how many times that's happened in front of your daughter? It's easy to see how young girls can get the impression that not only is every woman trying to lose weight, but every woman should be—and to do so gives you a certain status among other women. Just as our girls are figuring out what it means to be grown women, it makes sense that they're already trying to restrict calories, work out, and take off their brand-new extra pounds. After all, that's what women do.

What makes so many of us proudly tell our daughters how little we weighed at a certain time in our lives, as if that lower number was an accomplishment in and of itself? I can remember my mother showing me a picture of herself lying on the couch in our family's living room. She was wearing a black sweater with black-and-white checkered pants, and she was fast asleep. "I was 110 pounds then," she told me.

Later, I found out she was fast asleep on the couch—and 110 pounds—because she'd been ill for some time.

I thought of that picture as my Weight-Loss Diary came to an end. I reached my goal weight of 125 pounds in time for the November 2007 issue, and by the December issue, I was 121 pounds—four pounds below my goal weight. I'm sure many *Shape* readers were impressed that I'd finished the column well below goal. What the copy didn't say, however, was that my final weigh-in was done the week after I'd been released from the hospital after spending three days there, hooked up to IV fluids, incredibly sick with salmonella poisoning. I pictured readers everywhere chastising themselves for not being able to stick with their weight-loss programs and mimic my fantastic, go-beyond-goal results.

Twenty-four-year-old Melanie, not yet a mom, had a similar experience when she lost quite a bit of weight after having surgery for a vascular problem. She says she never thought of herself as heavy until people began to compliment her on her weight loss and tell her how terrific she looked.

"I was probably in a size 10 before the surgery," she tells me. "I wasn't thinking about dropping weight. But then everyone started telling me how wonderful I looked now that I was 130 pounds and a size 0. So I worked on keeping it off."

These days, Melanie is an assistant manager at a gym, competes in fitness competitions, and hopes to do some modeling for fitness magazines. She works hard at keeping her weight down through workouts and an eating plan that has her eating "clean, healthy" foods five times a day. Her body and how it looks are important to her, and she gives her appearance a lot of effort. So she's not immune to the comments that others make or to feeling bad about her weight.

"When you weigh too much, you feel bad because you weigh too much," she says. "But when you weigh too little and people make comments, you feel bad, too. It's almost like you can't win. You're never good enough. You have to find a weight that makes you happy so that when you look in the mirror, you're happy. You can't try to please everybody else because you never will."

Sophie says she wishes moms could know how much girls hate it when their mothers comment on their weight—even in a good way, like telling them they look as if they've lost a few pounds.

"Because when their mothers—the one person who is supposed to love them unconditionally—start judging them, it just adds even more pressure in a world where people are constantly looking at you and judging you on the way you look," she says.

Keeping Pounds in Perspective

I think about Sophie's words often—and I remind myself of them whenever Faith and I talk about weight. When the Weight-Loss Diary ended, I made the conscious decision not to buy a scale to keep tabs on my weight at home, even though that decision is contrary to much of the recommended research on people who successfully maintain weight loss. The National Weight Control Registry reports that 75 percent of people who've lost weight and maintained the loss for approximately five years weigh themselves at least once a week.[1] Clearly, the scale has some value when it comes to maintaining a healthy weight.

Sure, I want to maintain my new weight, but more importantly, I want to maintain my perspective. It's a situation where, once again, what I do matters just as much—if not more—than what I say. Even if I tell my daughter that weight is just a measurement and not the whole picture, that doesn't mean much if I'm constantly hopping on the scale and fretting about a pound up here or rejoicing about a pound down there.

Instead, Faith and I talk a lot about how we feel. Since we don't keep a scale at home, weight is simply an occasional measurement. When we shop, we talk a lot about how clothes are made and the fact that one manufacturer's size 0 may be equal to another's size 3. These numbers are subjective, and they don't tell the whole truth—instead, I want her to ask herself, "How do I feel? Am I taking good care of my body?" By asking myself those questions—and being honest about the answers—I hope I'm teaching her that *those* answers matter more than any measurement of pounds.

Dr. May, who counsels many people trying to lose weight in her weight-management programs, says that stepping on the scale too often can actually get in the way of weight-loss and weight-maintenance efforts, causing us to make choices we wouldn't normally make—from the classic "I ate right, but still didn't lose weight, so I might as well have a sundae" to "I've already weighed in for this week, so now it's time for a splurge"—based on the number we see. It's more important to focus on simply eating right most of the time and moving your body in some way every day. If you've done those things, you're more likely to be at peace with the scale—and to teach your daughter to be at peace with it, too.

A mom I know was recently telling me about her inability to lose those last four pounds she wanted to lose, in spite of exercising and watching what she eats. She looked startled when I said, "But you look terrific. So what does it matter?" I'll admit that I cringed when she told me a story about changing outfit after outfit, unable to find anything she didn't "feel fat" in, prompting her young daughter—who was watching the whole episode—to ask, "Mommy, what are you doing?"

"It all comes full circle," Dr. May tells me. "We pick things up as little kids, and we carry them with us. We don't even know that we've internalized those feelings; we just know that when we look in the mirror, we feel bad."

Leah, age twenty-seven, a newly married school-teacher who's not yet a mom, says her mother's example was instrumental in teaching her to have a healthy rela-tionship with her body. "Growing up, we never had a scale in the house," she tells me. "My mom would always tell me to go by how I felt and how my clothes felt on me. She never really commented on the way I looked; if I wanted to talk about my body, she'd let me start the discussion. She definitely helped me feel more comfort-able with my own body."

We can all learn something from the relaxed attitude of Leah's mom—mainly, not to judge ourselves, our daughters, or each other so harshly when it comes to something as inconsequential as a number on a scale. Carolyn, age forty-eight, thinks that home should be the safe place where no matter what you weigh, you know that people aren't going to reject you. As she puts it so eloquently, "Home has to be the place where you can just feel that people are going to love you no matter what shape your body's in."

Showing our girls that we accept them at any weight starts with showing them that we accept ourselves—no matter what the scale tells us.

Body Image Builders

As your daughter approaches adolescence, remind her that everyone's body is changing at this age and that she and her friends are not necessarily on the same growth schedule. For girls to compare their weights isn't fair to anybody. The only person she should be comparing herself to is herself! Actually, that's good advice for you, too; here are some tips to help keep her weight—and yours—in perspective:

Make health the priority. If your daughter's weight gain has you concerned, schedule a physical, and have the doctor advise you on good nutrition and exercise habits as part of overall good health. But don't let it be about weight.

Toss the scale—or at least hide it. If the temptation to step on the scale daily is too much, get rid of it. If you just have to know, weigh yourself at the gym or a friend's house, or stop in at the doctor's office once a month for a quick check of your status. But don't let your daughter see you obsessing over a number.

Get philosophical. If you're wearing the same size you've been wearing, you're taking good care of yourself, and you feel good, ask yourself why the number even matters. Remember, normal fluctuations can result from eating, exercise, and bathroom habits, as well as from regular hormonal changes. If you're truly gaining weight, chances are you'll see it in the way your clothes fit and can address it right away, so why worry about it?

Corral your compliments. Resist the urge to focus on weight when doling out compliments to friends and family. Let your daughter hear you tell a friend she looks fantastic or healthy or happy without it being about having lost weight.

6

If I Looked Like Her,
I'd Be Happy
Teaching Your Daughter to
Think Critically about Media

> I do photo shoots at home with my personal
> camera. I just love the expressions and being in
> front of the camera. My favorite model right
> now is Tyra Banks. She's really famous.
>
> —*Allison, age twelve*

It's Saturday afternoon, and the mail has just been
delivered to our house. In the stack I'm holding is
the latest issue of *Seventeen* magazine, featuring *Sisterhood of the Traveling Pants* star America Ferrera on its
cover. This can mean only one thing: I won't see my
daughter for the next hour or two.

I'm not exactly sure of when my own obsession with
magazines began—I have vague memories of my mom

occasionally reading a copy of *Family Circle*—but I do remember waiting rabidly for the mailman to deliver my latest copy of *Teen*. I'd curl up on the couch and devour every word and image on its glossy pages. These days, I often find Faith—who shares my magazine obsession—curled up with her own copies. Our mailbox is full of subscriptions to everything from *Shape* and *Self* to *Health* and *More*. She loves to page through just about every magazine I get, along with a few subscriptions of her own.

Parenting experts might say I should be doing everything in my power to shield my daughter from the media, but I disagree. The fact is, I'm a magazine writer, and magazines are part of our lives. Instead of harming her, I think I'm teaching her a valuable skill: how to separate fantasy from reality and how to fit what she sees and reads into a larger picture.

Sure, it might be nice if the only influence on the way our daughters feel about their bodies—and the way we feel about ours—was our own. But imagine a world without TV, movies, magazines, or the Internet. Boring! Sure, maybe there'd be no idealized images of female beauty for us to agonize over, but then there'd be no TV, movies, magazines, or websites either. I like my entertainment, thank you very much. I bet you do, too.

A quick online search will take you to countless studies about the harmful effects that media images can have on the body images of girls and women. In a recent article on raising girls with healthy self-esteem, Anita

Gurian, PhD, of the NYU Child Study Center mentions one survey that found that 59 percent of girls in grades five through twelve were dissatisfied with their body shape and that 47 percent said they wanted to lose weight because of magazine pictures.[1] At age ten, Gurian writes, 20 to 40 percent of girls have begun dieting. What's more, a 2007 study at the University of Missouri–Columbia found that after just three minutes of looking at pictures of models in magazine ads, the body images of all women in the study were equally and negatively affected, no matter what the women viewing the ads looked like.[2] And a 2006 study of girls between the ages of five and eight found that watching TV shows that focused on appearance had a negative influence on their body image and self-esteem.[3] Yikes! I don't deny the effects that these images can have, if girls are left alone with them. But what seems to be missing in the equation is context—and that's something every girl needs.

Faith and I have always talked about the magazine world in general, but when I took on *Shape*'s Weight-Loss Diary column, she got a true behind-the-scenes look at how words and images are shaped (no pun intended) to reflect what the magazine is selling—whether it's a philosophy, a lifestyle, a body image, or the products of its advertisers. Her first peek came when I let her read a column I'd written before I sent it to my editor. There was a line she liked, but when the column appeared in the magazine, the line had been changed.

"Hey," she said. "That's not what you wrote."

"Nope," I told her. "That's editing."

I could see the lights come on as she considered how my words had been changed to reflect what the *magazine* wanted me to say. Soon, she picked up on the photography, too. The photo *Shape* had chosen for my very first column made me "look bigger than you really are," according to Faith. "That's for dramatic effect," I told her. "The bigger I look at the beginning, the smaller I'll look at the end."

She quickly noticed other photographic discrepancies, too. In the March issue, she told me, my "teeth look whiter than usual" (I'm still trying to decide if I should feel insulted by that). But it was the May issue that really gave her a taste of what's behind the image on the page. The editors wanted her to appear in the photo with me, since the column was about how my mother's body image had affected my own and how mine was affecting Faith's. Hair, makeup, and styling for the shot took about two and a half hours. The photo, taken on a freezing January day in front of my neighbor's evergreen tree, appeared to be the picture of springtime lushness. I wish you could have seen the look on Faith's face when I joked with the photographer that the thin springtime sweater I was wearing was going to leave two, *ahem*, very visible indicators of the cold. "Don't worry," she cheerfully replied. "We'll just Photoshop them out." For Faith—and for me—the experience was a great lesson in the illusion of perfection.

It's a lesson I wish all girls could witness up close. Glamorous media images can be downright intoxicating at a time when girls are choosing who and what they want to be. Besides, they've been encouraged by us—their parents—to believe they can be anything, and it's natural that many want to be that girl they see on the page. What they've yet to understand, though, is *even the girl on the page isn't that girl.* As moms, it's up to us to help them see that.

An Altered Reality

I don't think it's possible to insulate girls from the media, and I'm not sure that we'd want to. Pop culture, news, the latest movies, and the hottest songs are pretty much what teens talk about, when they're not talking about each other, of course. Rather than trying to shut out the images that bombard our daughters every day, we're better off teaching them to become "media smart"—to develop their own filter through which they can run what they see and hear, before they start thinking about how they measure up to those models and celebrities.

"I'm definitely a victim of reading magazines and feeling horrible about my weight when I see models or actresses," says twenty-seven-year-old Leah. "I'd like to have Eva Longoria's legs or Cameron Diaz's arms. Sometimes I talk to my mom about people in the magazines, and she says I have to remember that those people have a whole staff dedicated to making them look good."

Leah's mom is right. Not only do celebrities and models have a staff—like personal chefs, trainers, stylists, makeup artists, and publicists—dedicated to making them look good in real life, they've also got people working behind the scenes to improve the images the rest of us see. Just ask Tonya Schwartz, who works as a photo retoucher in the fashion magazine industry and for retail print advertising. For the last thirteen years, she's spent eight hours a day fixing skin blemishes, erasing pores, lengthening limbs, increasing bust size, and shaping booty. All so that the rest of us will want to buy whatever her client is selling.

"Whenever we have a tour in my company and kids are around, I always show them the before and after pictures of people," she says. "I want them to know that this is make-believe. There's no reality here. We're not trying to reflect what women actually look like; we're trying to enhance the good parts and make things sell."

As adults, we may be able to recognize when we're being manipulated, but it's a bit tougher for our girls, who may be more inclined to believe that the right product or right "look" will magically make their lives better. Take fifteen-year-old Tammy, for instance, who tells me, "I wish my mom knew that I wouldn't ask for the new face wash and makeup if I didn't feel I needed it to be happy."

Helping our daughters understand that what they're seeing isn't the real thing is the first step in teaching them to think critically about media images. With Faith, I take a practical approach, explaining that advertisers pay lots of money to have their products appear in a magazine and, because of that, they're going to spend lots of time and money making sure that the person in the ad looks so perfect that all the magazine's readers want to look like her—and think that using the advertiser's product will help them do that. Not only does the girl in the ad probably not really look like that, chances are, she probably doesn't even use that product.

We also like to poke around on the Web together, looking at sites like Dove's Campaign for Real Beauty, which features films showing behind-the-scenes "tricks" used at photo shoots and the level of digital retouching that goes into a magazine photo. Yes, I've heard the argument that it's hypocritical for a company that makes and sells beauty products to create such a campaign, but I do applaud Dove's willingness to shine a light on these manipulative practices. The bottom line is that it's healthy for our daughters—and for us moms—to see and understand just how they're being deceived.

Play "Find the Flaws"

Once you've talked with your daughter about how media images aren't a reflection of what real women look like, try a fun game of "find the flaws" to prove it to her—she'll soon see that in print images, you'll rarely find any.

To play, have her look at a real photograph, and then compare it to a magazine image. If you don't see any shadows under the eyes or around one side of the nose or the other in the magazine photo, you're likely looking at a retouched image, says Tonya Schwartz. Other clues include flawless skin without pores, missing creases in the lips, and eyes that look like they're one solid color instead of varying shades. Another place to look is at hands and feet—no visible wrinkles at the knuckles and no visible veins are a pretty good indicator of retouching.

Of course, we can talk all day about teaching our daughters to look at magazine images with a skeptical eye, but if we can't convince ourselves to stop comparing our own bodies to them, we'll never convince our daughters to stop, either. You might not think so, but your daughter also takes her cues about the importance of media images from you.

Take Colleen, for example. At forty, she's the mom of three daughters ages thirteen, eleven, and six. An avid magazine reader, Colleen often doesn't like the way she looks when she sees herself in a photograph. After her pregnancies, she really struggled with comparing herself to celebrities who seemed to effortlessly drop weight and get their pre-baby bodies back immediately after giving birth. "I admire the styles that a lot of celebrities are able to wear," she says. "Dressing up is a frustrating experience when I feel overweight."

Although Colleen says she wants to model positive feelings about her body for her daughters, it's tough for her to stop comparing herself to these images. Abby, age forty-two, reports a similar experience. She often watches *America's Next Top Model* with her fifteen-year-old daughter. "We talk a lot about how they're just too skinny," she says. "But unfortunately, I think we do compare ourselves to the girls we see on TV."

Those kinds of comparisons don't do anybody any good. Although they're certainly real, celebrities and reality television stars don't exactly fall into the same category most moms do when it comes to their bodies. Again, though, it's a matter of context. Pick up the newspaper or turn on the TV to hear the story of the latest eating-disordered celebrity, and you'll soon figure out that the fantasy world of film and television brings with it real-world pressures to be thin that you and I don't face in our everyday lives. Most of us aren't being photographed or filmed in our jobs, and it's important for our girls to understand the depths that celebrities with "ideal" bodies have to go to—staying unnaturally thin so they'll look their "best" on camera.

A few years ago, Faith and I went to a family birthday party at a local roller-skating rink. We were in the arcade playing Skee Ball when she suddenly pulled on my arm. "Mom, isn't that lady on TV?" she asked in a loud stage whisper. I turned to look, and a few feet away stood a local news anchorwoman—or at least the shell of her. She looked like a bobblehead doll of herself.

"She doesn't look like she does on TV," Faith said. "She doesn't look right."

Later, I explained to her that the camera tends to add weight to people's frames so movie and TV stars have to stay extra thin so they'll look thin on camera. And by extra thin, I mean downright skeletal. I wish every girl could attend a photo shoot or see a favorite celebrity up close sometime. I can virtually guarantee that she'd be shocked at just how thin many of these people actually are.

It's all part of the illusion of perfection. Melissa, my dietitian for *Shape*'s Weight-Loss Diary column, says she hates seeing TV shows and magazines that make girls feel bad about themselves. "When you look around you in everyday life, how many people do you see that actually look like people in magazines or on TV? You don't," she says. Meanwhile, "a lot of people set an ideal weight or 'look' for themselves based on what they find in magazines."

Creating a New Ideal

So what can we as moms do to make sure that our daughters aren't getting hung up on comparing themselves to a girl that doesn't even exist?

Consider your own media consumption.

First up is an awareness check of our own relationship with the media. Normally, I'd never encourage people to give up reading magazines (it's my livelihood, after all), but if you find that certain kinds of magazines do nothing but make you feel bad about yourself, why read them? If, in spite of all you know about photo retouching, you still find yourself wistfully wanting to look just like the woman on the page and berating yourself for not doing it, it's time to subscribe to some new titles.

Talk to your daughter about what she sees.

If you're able to be more analytical, though, you're in a great position to encourage your daughter to think critically about what she sees. By the time a girl is in elementary school, she's already been thinking about her body and how she measures up to those around her, according to Dr. Andrea Vazzana of the NYU Child Study Center. Now is the time to talk to her about what she's seeing. By the time they're ready for middle school, most girls are capable of grasping the concept of photo retouching, wise enough to know that it happens, and aware enough to understand the pressure that these images can put on them.

Fifteen-year-old Sophie put it best when she told me, "The pressure to be thin, but not too thin, definitely comes from the media. I mean, there's always a part of us that wants to believe that magazines and tabloids are just stupid, but the reality is we're constantly criticizing ourselves."

We moms can help buffer that constant wave of criticism that chips away at our girls. It's all in the approach. Tonya Schwartz suggests teaching girls to look at media images the same way we'd teach them to look at a portrait in a museum or gallery. You know it's not real; it's a representation of the artist's own ideal image of beauty, and chances are, you're not expecting yourself to measure up to that particular artist's ideal.

Let her know that photographs are just that—photographs.

That same logic can work when we're paging through our favorite magazines, too. Looking at the images as just that—images—and looking for evidence of retouching teach girls not to simply accept what they see as the truth. Often we get distracted because advertisements and photo spreads are designed to highlight a model's one good feature. The human parts that would make you realize this person is simply human get removed before you look at the shot, says Schwartz. "Your eyes get trained to not see reality as reality," she says. "When you're reading magazines, you just start to see the painted reality."

It all sounds good in theory, doesn't it? But what do you do if your daughter comes to you in tears because her arms aren't as willowy as those of her favorite TV star? You can gently remind her that those willowy arms come with a price tag—maybe hours in the gym that leave her no time for friends, or maybe an eating disorder that has her hating herself. But tread carefully; if your daughter has a heavy case of hero worship, she might not take kindly to you "criticizing" her idol. You may think her favorite star is sickly thin, but instead of pointing that out, you might try gently broaching the topic with a more casual observation about the toll that stardom might be taking on her idol. Rather than wondering aloud why on earth your daughter would want arms so thin they look like they could snap in two at any second, you might try a more subtle, "Wow, it must be hard for her to stay so thin. I wonder what it's like to be under so much pressure." That way, you've shown support for your daughter's idol, but also opened the door to a conversation about not only the pressures stars face to stay so very thin, but the unnatural images portrayed on TV. These are the kinds of conversations that get girls talking about the pressures they feel in their own lives, too.

Of course, girls who are naturally slender are also feeling body image pressure from the media, too. Lately, magazines and tabloid television have fixated on celebrities they consider "too thin." We've all been in line at the supermarket checkout and seen tabloid covers accusing slim celebrities like Keira Knightley, Nicole Ritchie, and the Olsen twins of having eating disorders. Maybe they do, or maybe they don't, but now many girls are feeling the pressure of the media's demands that they be neither too heavy nor too thin.

"I can't even count the number of times I've been accused of being anorexic," Sophie tells me. "It's so annoying when people accuse girls of [having] eating disorders. I mean, aren't thin people supposed to be the envied ones? If you can't be too fat and you can't be too thin, when do we catch a break?"

When, indeed?

Media images can have a huge impact on our daughters' developing body image, says Dr. Vazzana. "Parents should start talking to their children in elementary school, when they're about seven, eight, or nine years old," she says. "That's when these messages start sinking in with kids. You need to encourage kids to make critical judgments and to acknowledge that not everyone can look like a model or even should look like a model."

What's most important, she adds, is that we moms challenge the images that are presented to us and to our girls in magazines, on television, and even on billboards. Our girls need to know that healthy—and beautiful—bodies come in all shapes and sizes, but they won't learn that from the media. It's our lesson to teach.

Body Image Builders

Media is a huge part of our lives, but you don't need to shield your daughter to mitigate its negative effects on her body image. Talk to her about what she's seeing, reading, and listening to, and teach her not to simply accept it all as reality. Here's how:

Mind your own media. Stay aware of your behavior and how you respond to media images. She'll take her cues from you.

Mind her media, too. Keep tabs on what she's watching and reading. If she loves *Gossip Girl* or *90210*, sit and watch it with her. If she likes to read magazines, flip through the pages, or glance at the table of contents, to get a sense of what she's absorbing.

Keep conversation casual. Ask her about her favorite stars or models, and find out what she likes about them. Use these opportunities to start a deeper conversation about media images if the moment seems right.

Develop an artist's eye. Help her spot the ways that images have been manipulated and retouched to change what's really there.

Don't "diss" her idols. She may consider her favorite stars her "friends." Keep that in mind when you're tempted to comment or criticize.

Mean Girls and Frenemies
When Our Bodies Become Targets

> Generally, when a friend doesn't like the way
> something looks on you, she won't say it out-
> right. However, a snide look or a sideways glance
> can hurt your feelings just as much.
>
> —*Grace, age fifteen*

I was thirteen when my body really started to change. It was the summer between seventh and eighth grade, and I remember being thrilled to finally have something to fill the bra I'd been wearing for a couple of years. Shopping for new clothes that August, I noticed I'd gone up a size or two, but it was no big deal to me. I looked forward to getting back to school, anxious to reconnect with some of the friends I hadn't seen all summer. On the first day, I searched the hallways for my pals, and we soon moved as a pack, certain that things would be as they'd always been.

But they weren't.

Girls in school began to whisper to each other about who was fat, who liked whom, and who thought she was better than everybody else. I tried to ignore the whispers, but secretly I started to worry that I was the fat one. At thirteen, being different from my friends, with their coltish legs and tiny waists, seemed like the end of my adolescent world. One afternoon, I returned to the locker room after gym class to find a standard-issue brown school paper towel on top of my neatly folded clothes. I picked it up, and scrawled in black marker was "YRUFAT?"

Why are you fat?

My face burned with shame as I got dressed, headed back to class, and prayed to make it through the day without letting whoever had written it see me cry.

In the weeks that followed, I started paying more at-tention to the "who's fat" chatter. I stared into the mirror, sucking in my stomach and straining to catch a glimpse of my behind. The powerful legs I'd once appreciated— the ones that let me flip higher and execute a perfect back handspring—now seemed enormous, and, even worse, they'd started to jiggle. My clothes didn't seem to fit right either; squirming into my freshly laundered jeans was a major struggle. My friends began a daily compari-son of how much they weighed, and the one with the lowest number was declared that day's unspoken winner. "Ninety-nine pounds," one would tell the group. "Oh," another would say sadly. "I'm 103."

I didn't weigh myself at first, but before long, I couldn't stand not knowing how I measured up. One afternoon, while my mom was at work, I dragged the dust-covered scale out from under the bathroom sink and stepped on it: 135. Twenty-five pounds more than most of my friends.

That was the beginning of my obsession—and of my teenage self-loathing.

As an adult, I now know that what was happening to my body was normal. We've all heard about the "awkward phase" that young teens go through, and that was simply mine. It wasn't obesity; it wasn't even necessarily a problem. But at that age, to me, it was a tragedy of epic proportions. To be different—and to be called out as being different—from my friends was almost unbearable in a world filled with crowded hallways, passed notes, and lunchroom politics.

Most of us have our own awful adolescent memories—times when we felt teased, shamed, or put down because of the way our bodies looked or what we were wearing. You know that old expression about the more things change, the more they stay the same? Our girls are collecting their own memories, too:

"Sometimes, other girls call me fat. It's usually when they're around their friends—and it's people that I don't even know, too. Moms don't really understand as much as they think they do about being in the community of girls that we have to be in. These girls, at least the ones I go to school with, can be malicious and evil. Of all the stories my mom tells me about her younger years, I've never heard one that had to do with girls as mean as the ones I see and hear from every day."—Amanda, age thirteen

"My breasts are big, and even though I'm OK with my breasts, I've been bullied about it. One mean girl asked me if it was true that I stuff my bra. I don't tell my mom because I'm afraid she'd have me do something weird. If I had a friend who didn't like her body, I would send her nameless notes giving her advice."—Laurie, age ten

"People are like, 'Is that a boy or a girl?' and laugh at me. They never speak directly to me. But my friends have said they like what I wear and the way I look. I believe my really close friends because I trust them."—Katherine, age fourteen

In the social world of adolescent girls, differences in body size and shape are a magnet for other insecure girls looking to cement their own place in the pack. There's no denying that some girls are outright nasty, but even friends seem to morph into mean girls when we least expect it. It's a complicated world, and one that often leaves us moms crying our own tears when we see our daughters in so much pain.

Not Good Enough

Whether it starts with a comment from someone else or with simply sizing herself up, a budding awareness of

how her body looks different from those of her friends—
or even from how it *used* to look—can often spark feelings of being "not good enough" in girls.

"My mom says I could be a model," says Michaela, age
twelve, who's taller than many of the girls—and boys—
in her class. "But I wish she knew that I think I'm a little
too big."

It's those kind of peer comparisons, along with comparisons to digitally distorted media images, that have
our girls wondering if they're OK as they are. When I
think back to my own early teenage years and my feelings about my body, it's as if someone had pulled the rug
out from under me. One moment, I was a happy-go-
lucky kid running around and eating whatever I pleased.
The next, I was a "fat girl" who dreaded gym class and
thought about skipping lunch. What hurt most was that
I couldn't figure out what I'd done "wrong" to become
that girl.

That feeling—that you've done something wrong or
are somehow "less than" because of the way your changing (or not yet changing) body looks—is at the heart of
relational victimization (or "girl bullying," as it's sometimes called). Girls this age are incredibly sensitive, not
only about their bodies, but about any ways they see
themselves as different from their peers. Girls with dominant personalities or more powerful social status can
quickly hone in on a weaker (or socially threatening) girl's
area of body sensitivity and use it as a source of ridicule

and power. And because other girls don't want to become the target of teasing, they're often all too quick to jump on the bandwagon, further strengthening the dominant girl's status.

As adults, it's easy for us to see how the downward spiral happens: Whether it's true or not, young adolescents are more likely to believe what other people say about them. A girl who feels just fine about her body, but then "overhears" a classmate say that she's fat or flat-chested or ugly, will likely be looking harder at herself in the mirror tomorrow.

Sometimes even an "innocent" comment from a friend about the outfit she's wearing can send a girl's body image into a tailspin. "You can have this great self-image, and then one person will say one little thing, and it makes you think, 'Why would they say that?'" says Melanie, age twenty-four. "It completely changes you. You're like, 'Wait, maybe I'm not OK.'"

Remember thirty-seven-year-old Cindy, whose mother had been quite heavy throughout her childhood and teen years and therefore tried to control what Cindy ate so she wouldn't get fat, too? Though her mother was telling her she weighed too much, Cindy now looks back and remembers going with a friend to his prom—and the size 7 dress she wore at the time.

"My friends were wearing a size 0. I had an hourglass figure in the seventh grade, but they were all stick figures," she tells me. "I was shaped differently, so I was beating myself up for nothing—and I was getting beat up by my mother for nothing. I mean, I wasn't over-weight. I was over *their* weight."

The seeds of feeling bad about our bodies often get planted when we first begin to notice the ways that we're different from our peers. And because girls' bodies are changing so rapidly in adolescence—and at different rates—it's not uncommon for girls to feel out of sync, de-velopmentally, when comparing themselves to their friends. No one wants to be the last one to grow breasts, but that doesn't mean anyone wants to be the first, either.

Maura, age thirty-seven, says her twelve-year-old daughter had a pool party during the summer and invited five girls to come. "It was amazing," she tells me. "They were all different shapes and sizes. One looked like she was about seventeen—totally developed, thin, and tall—and another was about twenty pounds overweight. Then there was everything in between; they were just very dif-ferently shaped twelve-year-old bodies."

The fact that girls often look so different at this age—at a time when they most desperately want to look the same—makes comparisons a particularly tricky area for moms to address. Faith has some friends who still look like little girls and others who look like grown women. She's not sure who she should be measuring herself against at this point, and frankly, I can remember *my* mother trying to reassure me that my friends and I would all even out in the end. Sometimes, it was comforting, but other times, I was convinced that she just didn't get what it was like to be a girl my age.

Funny, isn't it? If you're anything like me, I'm willing to bet you can reconnect with your adolescent angst at a moment's notice. I'm sure that my mom could. So how do we now convince our daughters that we "get it"?

"Mom, You Don't Understand . . ."

As moms, we do understand all this. We've been there. And that's exactly why it hurts so much. Watching our girls begin to struggle with the way they feel about their bodies is just about one of the hardest things for moms to witness—especially if we've spent a lifetime struggling with our own bad body feelings. Now there's scientific evidence that old hurts die hard: A 2008 University of Florida study found that relational victimization in adolescence is linked to depression and anxiety in early adulthood.[1] Those old hurts can often play out in our relationships with our daughters and in what we teach them about their bodies. An old friend of mine, teased and left out as a young teen, was forever telling me that she wasn't going to allow what was done to her to be done to her daughter.

Because so many of us developed our own body image issues during adolescence, it can feel like we're stepping back in time when we have to watch our daughters endure the same things we did. Our maternal instinct is to protect them from the harm we received, whether by lashing out at those who tease them or by trying to "prevent" them from becoming targets in the first place.

Ah, but that's the tricky part, isn't it?

We can't fully protect our daughters from other girls' comments or mean behavior. We can't be so afraid that our daughters will become the "fat girl" who gets teased that we become overly controlling, as Cindy's mom did, or worse, give our daughters the idea that the normal weight they're gaining is, in fact, something to be ashamed of and avoided. And we have to be really careful that we don't project our own memories of teen hurts onto what our daughters are experiencing—in fact, some studies have shown that moms who have anxious or negative memories of their own peer experiences tend to have kids who are rejected by their peers, says Dr. Mitch Prinstein, associate professor and director of clinical psychology, who studies peer relationships in the Peer Relations Lab at the University of North Carolina at Chapel Hill. Because of this, moms can sometimes interpret ambiguous experiences that happen to their kids as hostile, he says.

It's hard to watch our girls suffer hostility—real or perceived—at the hands of other girls. "There have been the mean girls—you know, the popular girls at that age, and they've called her names," says Karin, mom to Amanda, who struggles with her weight. "But she has friends, and I don't believe the friends that have been here and that she hangs with have ever said anything to her. But I don't think she would open up and tell me at this point. At this age, she probably thinks more in-wardly about it or talks to her friends."

When your daughter is being teased or hurt by other girls, it's so tempting to want to jump to her defense. "Some of Laurie's friends call her a weakling," says Lisa. "Laurie does ballet, and her friends are all on a swim team, and they think ballet is nothing. What they don't realize is that Laurie is just as strong, if not stronger, than [they are]."

Lisa's indignation is understandable. But we can't march into school and demand that the other girls be nice to our daughter. So what can we do to buoy our girls against the hurt caused by bullies?

Share, Care, and Stay Aware

You may not be able to make relational bullying stop, but you can mitigate its effects.

Share stories from your own adolescence.

Start by being willing to share your own stories of ado-lescent pain with your daughter if she wants to hear them, or enlist the help of an older friend or relative your daughter respects. Sometimes, it just helps to know that other people have gone through similar experiences and survived. But don't expect the "I got through it, so you will, too" approach to magically make things better for your daughter.

"It's really hard for kids to be able to take that future perspective," says Dr. Prinstein. "They're so focused on the present situation—they only see the here and now."

**Let her know you're there
for her if she wants to talk.**

Though she may not be able to convince herself that all this will pass, it's good to let your daughter know that you're always willing to listen and that you won't simply brush off what she tells you as "kids being kids."

Point out the "why."

When I was a young teen, my mother was very big on exploring the "why" behind other people's behavior. She always listened, and through my conversations with her, I learned to recognize when other people's comments, faces, gestures, and behaviors really had nothing to do with me—it was more about them and their insecurities.

That's important, says Dr. Prinstein. He says it's helpful to talk with girls about what's happening and to help them understand that this kind of bullying doesn't have anything to do with who they are as people, nor will it last forever. Eighty percent of kids experience some sort of victimization in adolescence, he says; those who don't internalize it—in other words, girls who learn to say, "Suzy's just picking on me because she saw Brian talking to me in the hall and she's jealous," instead of, "Suzy's picking on me because I'm fat and ugly"—stand a much better chance of not carrying the effects of bullying—and a bad body image—with them into adulthood.

Still, understanding the "why" is small comfort to a girl who's on the receiving end of this behavior and has to endure it. I've been working hard with Faith to help her understand that just because somebody says something doesn't mean it's true. We're also working on the "so what" strategy. Now when someone tells her she's short or makes fun of her braces, she's learning to tell them (and herself), "So what?"

Expect conformity.

It's also important for moms to understand girls' need for conformity at this age. (Remember leg warmers? Fingerless gloves? Socks over the jeans and upturned collars? Need I say more?) Though it may be contrary to everything we want to tell them—be yourself, do your own thing, wear what looks good on *your* body—the reality is, fitting in with your peers is usually about being just like them. I may not think a certain clothing style is the most flattering to Faith's figure, but if that's what all her friends are wearing, I try to remember what it was like to need to be the same as everybody else. If a bit of fashion conformity gives her the self-confidence she'll need to say no to more dangerous peer pressures, then I'm all for it.

Abby's fifteen-year-old daughter, Tammy, is very self-conscious about being taller and a bit bigger than most of her friends, so Abby tries to do what she can to help Tammy make the most of her appearance. "It gets expensive, but I really try to make sure that her clothes fit her nicely and that her hair is cut nicely," she tells me. "I try to make sure she's not saying, 'I'd be fine if I just had this pair of jeans that fit me right.'"

Pam has taken a similar approach with her twelve-year-old daughter, Allison.

"I did decide to buy her some clothes from Abercrombie so she would feel like she fit in and [could] relax, and I hope now she can think about schoolwork instead of worrying that she's wearing the wrong stuff," she says. "When I was young, wearing brand-name Levi's was *the* thing. I remember how good it felt to own one pair."

When Conformity Goes Too Far

Sure, we need to remember how important it is to our girls that they fit in with their friends. But we also have to be on the lookout for those times when conformity goes too far. There have always been—and always will be—cliques or groups that separate girls from each other;

some are healthy, like math club or the basketball team. Others, like groups that "require" girls to maintain a certain weight or perform certain acts with boys, can damage not only body image but mental and physical health. Last year, an uproar broke out when newspapers in Australia reported the existence at a Catholic high school of "Club 21," a group of girls whose members were said to wear wrist bracelets that displayed their ranking—from one to twenty-one—based on their looks, thinness, and popularity with boys.[2]

Though it's rare for groups to be so organized, most girls are well aware of who the popular girls are and whether or not they fit into that group. If you look closely at girl cliques, you'll find that most of the members are likely to share a similar body type. A study on friendship cliques and peer influences on body image published in the *Journal of Pediatric Psychology* found that groups of girl friends often share body image concerns[3]— in other words, girls who hang out together are likely not only to have similar ideas about what the "perfect" body looks like, but also to share similar behaviors in trying to achieve it (exercise, dieting, etc.).

Jealousy also runs rampant in girl cliques—even among good friends. "They're all focused on what they're wearing, and you can't wear the same type of thing," Abby says, talking about her daughter Tammy's group of friends. "And Tammy has this beautiful long hair and big boobs. That issue comes up all the time. Her friends will sometimes say stuff like, 'Oh, you should cut your hair.' But my husband's sister is really close to Tammy, and she's a very tell-it-like-it-is auntie. She'll say, 'That's what all the jealous girls say, honey. Don't cut your hair. They're jealous of your boobs, so they want you to cut your hair. Give it a week, and if you still want to cut it, cut it then.' And Tammy will end up saying, 'Oh, I don't want to cut my hair.' It's little stuff like that."

As adults, we've learned (or not) how to stand up for ourselves, and our girls need to learn how to stand up for themselves, too—usually on their own. But when the bullying is based on "flaws" in her body, it's more important than ever for your daughter to feel that she has your support. One way you can help her feel better about her changing body is to teach her to look critically not only at herself but also at others—including her tormentors. Just as you taught her to be smart about media images by looking for signs of digital enhancement, help her learn to look objectively at other girls' bodies. Have her name one attractive quality about a friend's body or appearance, then name one quality that isn't so attractive. Be clear—it's not about tearing other girls down; it's about recognizing that we all have some things about us that are beautiful and some things about us that we might wish we could change. It's a way to level the playing field, so to speak, when your daughter is being targeted by other girls. It works wonders for moms who feel intimidated by other women, too.

That strategy is one that Melissa, my *Shape* dietitian, has used over the years—both with clients and with herself.

"I don't care who you talk to, there's not a person in the world who doesn't have some sort of issues," she tells me. "If there's something that bothers you or you don't feel as good as somebody—and this is something I've learned to teach myself—look at them, and picture yourself being them, and imagine what your faults would be. What would be something that would bother you about yourself?"

By acknowledging that we all have things about our bodies—and ourselves—that we'd like to change, but that we like ourselves anyway, we show our girls by example that perfection isn't a requirement of good friendships, dating, marriage, a great job, or a mother's love.

"You know how your mother makes you feel that you're the best and the brightest?" says Susan, forty-four, mom to three girls ages fourteen, eleven, and seven. "Adolescents need that, I think. They need to believe that their mothers think the sun rises and sets on them. I don't like the way my daughter dresses because I just don't like teenage clothes right now. But I try to overlook it because it's not permanent and it's not harmful. It's an expression of who she is right now—I don't like her clothing, but I like her, and I like who she's becoming."

When we find ways to like and celebrate who our girls are—as Susan does—we teach them that they're

more than just a weight or a size or a shape. We teach
them that they're a whole person, with qualities and talents and strength. And by liking and celebrating ourselves and our own bodies, we teach them not to be
afraid to show the world that they like who they are—
and that's strong medicine against any mean girl.

Body Image Builders

Adolescence can be a tricky time for girls socially; as they begin to compare their bodies to those of their peers and looks become more important, appearance-based bullying, teasing, and shaming all rear their ugly heads. Here's how to help your daughter keep her cool when friends behave badly:

Help her *feel* that she looks her best. You may not love her style of dress, but as long as it's not dangerous or inappropriate, it's best to let her be. Make it your goal to help her feel confident among her peers.

Draw her out. Friends are so important to teens; it's natural for your daughter to pull away from you a bit. But if things aren't going well and you notice she's withdrawing, make time to do one of her favorite activities with her. Keep your connection strong so she knows she can always come to you.

Play to her strengths. Support her activities, hobbies, and talents so she has lots of positive things to feel good about beyond appearance.

Help her develop multiple friendship groups. Make sure she has lots of opportunities to get to know kids outside of school, whether through religious organizations, clubs, sports teams, or other interests. If she's being picked on in one group, having other friends helps keep her from internalizing the bullying.

PART 3

Mixed Messages

The Words We Use

When What You Say Shapes How She Feels

> I hate it when my mom calls me a lumberjack
> because I'm tall and sort of strong. It's just a joke,
> but it gets old fast.
>
> —*Katherine, age fourteen*

Teaching our daughters to stand up to bullies who say unkind things about them and their bodies is a valuable skill, for sure. But what about those times when we're the ones doing damage with the words we say—or don't say—to our girls, even if that's not our intention? Whether we're talking about our own bodies or theirs, there are lots of reasons why we say the things we do, and they're not always pretty. One thing is certain, though: Virtually no communication is more loaded—and more open to misinterpretation and downright frustration—than that between a mother and her teenage daughter.

Let me take you back to my own early teen years, when I began to torture my poor mother endlessly with cries of "Mom, am I fat? Do my legs look big?" She tried to reassure me with carefully chosen words: "You're sturdy." "You've got muscles." "You're athletic." The more I asked, the more she didn't say the three simple words I so desperately needed her to say:

"You're not fat."

My mom didn't say much about the pounds accumulating on my almost five-foot frame. But the fact that she wouldn't come right out and say what I needed to hear had me convinced at the time that she thought I was huge—even though she was way too busy serving as the target of her own jokes to criticize me. I hated those jokes, though other people seemed to think she was a riot. Sure, she was a few pounds overweight, but I didn't see what she thought was so unforgivable. Through her words and example, I adopted the family mantra: "If you think you're fat, you are." And though my mind—and some girls at school—was telling me I was, I didn't want to believe it. I wanted her to tell me it wasn't true.

But she didn't. And it took a long time to forgive her for that.

As an adult and a mom myself, I've had plenty of time to reflect on the whole thing, and here's what I think: Nobody wants their mom to lie to them. But maybe we don't exactly want her to tell us the truth, either. In the teenage world of constant comparisons and feeling as if we don't measure up, maybe all we really want to know is that our mom thinks we're OK, exactly as we are.

I was reminded of just how vulnerable a time this is for girls when Faith and I searched for a new bathing suit for her for a recent coed swim party. She had her heart set on a two-piece suit with a boy-short bottom. We searched some online shopping sites until she found her "perfect" suit—an adorable brown boy-shorts-bottom two-piece with bright blue trim. Knowing that style of bottom is a tough cut on my own curvy body, but determined to learn from my hurtful comment to Faith during the dinner roll incident, I bit my tongue, hoped for the best, and placed the order.

She couldn't wait for the suit to arrive; she knew she'd look perfect in it. She told all her friends about it, and some of them said they were going to get new suits for the party, too. Every day, she'd beg me to log on and check the tracking number to see exactly where her suit was.

As the days passed, my sense of dread grew stronger. She knew this was the perfect suit, and she was going to look perfect at the party. Again, I bit my tongue. Maybe it would be a perfect fit, and she'd step happily into the pool in front of all her friends. Maybe this suit would be the first brick in building a confident adolescent.

When the soft-pack envelope finally arrived in the mailbox, you'd have thought it was Christmas morning. She tore it open, ran to her room, and slammed the door. Minutes later, she emerged silently and stood in front of me. A single tear ran down her cheek.

"Oh, honey" was all I said. Then the floodgates opened, and she sobbed.

It was all wrong. She was all wrong, she said.

When we hit the stores the next day, I was determined to prove to her that it was the suit that was wrong—not her body. Instead of directing her to the "right" suit for her body type and thus pointing out what she'd surely forever see as her flaws—as my mother would have done in an attempt to help—I said, "Let's just try on as many suits as we can. Grab anything in your size that you like the color of, and let's give it a try." Twelve suits later, she emerged from the fitting room with a lovely two-piece suit with a little skirted bottom that looked absolutely adorable on her. Most important, though, was that she thought it looked adorable.

"You were right, Mom," she said. "I didn't like this on the hanger. Sometimes, you do have to just try things on."

Ah, sweet escape!

I'd emerged unscathed from this first major test of adolescent body angst. But I'm not foolish enough to think it'll always go this smoothly. Worrying about how she looks is something new for Faith—and her worry is something new for me. As mothers, we need to remember what it's like to be preoccupied with what we're wearing, how we look in it, and how it compares to what everybody else is wearing. And then we need to remember that well-meaning comments can easily be taken as criticism and that the hurt from a "joke" can last for years.

What Does That Mean?

The volatile nature of adolescence itself pretty much means that anything we say can and will be taken the wrong way. I cringe sometimes when Faith asks my opinion of an outfit she's put together; we both know that she doesn't want to hear that it would really look better with a belt or that I think she should wear the other shoes. I've said both of those things to her on occasion and been met with eye rolls, sighs, and watery eyes. Who knew a belt or shoes could be such a loaded topic?

Actually, I knew.

I can remember when the slightest suggestion from my mother felt like stinging criticism, and actual criticism felt like a vicious attack on everything I was. One Halloween, when I was about fourteen, I decided to make up my eyes with purple eye shadow and black liner to match the purple-and-black outfit I was wearing. It made perfect sense to me; it was Halloween, and that was the closest I'd come to a costume at that age. When I walked out into the kitchen, though, my mother took one look at me and said, "Um, that's an awful lot of eye shadow."

Sigh. Eye roll. Door slam. She just didn't get it.

Comments about my clothes were even worse, although in retrospect, I know she wasn't trying to hurt my feelings. I hated being told that something I was wearing "wasn't flattering" or that a different top "might look better" with those jeans. Fairly benign comments, wouldn't you say? But at that age, they weren't simply helpful suggestions. They were criticisms—of me and my body.

When Moms and Girls Compete

Of course, sometimes mothers make comments that aren't so benign.

"My mother was fairly direct and blunt about how she viewed you," Carolyn, age forty-eight, tells me. "She didn't tease you; she would come right out and say, 'You shouldn't eat that. You're fat.' If you'd ordered a cheeseburger, she'd say, 'Why don't you have a salad?' right in front of the waiter. I don't think she thought she was being insensitive or a bad parent—she just said stuff like that."

With her own daughters, Carolyn tries very hard not to make comments that could be hurtful. "Rarely, but occasionally, I've had to throw down the gauntlet and say, 'You cannot wear those pants; those pants are just too tight,' or 'You cannot go to school with skin showing,'" she says.

Looking back, Carolyn says, some of her mother's comments came from a place of competitiveness. Her mom and her mom's group of friends were very thin, she tells me, and they all smoked, drank, and put a lot of emphasis on femininity and sexuality. "Most of the women were stay-at-home housewives, and the whole thing about whether you were attractive to men was a huge way that women measured up," she says. "It was how they measured themselves against each other. I can remember her talking very viciously—almost gleefully—about a friend who'd gained ten pounds."

Liz, a fifty-year-old mother of three daughters, says she learned early on not to compete with her mother's appearance because she felt that she couldn't measure up. "I call my relationship with her, 'mirror, mirror on the wall,'" she says. "When she was young, my mother was a very beautiful, very striking woman. But there was always this underlying competition. What stands out most for me was that we went to the mall one time, and somebody said to her, 'You have a very beautiful daughter.' And she said, 'What, do you need glasses?' I was about fourteen or fifteen at the time, and it really hurt. I'll never forget it."

Today, Liz is philosophical about her mother's behavior. Appearance was very important to her, Liz says, because it brought her a lot of attention and made her special in the blue-collar working world her parents faced every day—attractiveness was a form of power. She was forever pointing out that she wore a size 7; even when Liz was an adult, she says, her mom would try to give her hand-me-down clothes. "She'd always say, 'This is size 7,'" she says. "It mattered to her a lot. She always wanted the focus to be on her."

Competitiveness also rears its ugly head sometimes in sibling relationships—especially if one daughter is constantly praised for her appearance, but the other isn't. Susan, age forty-four, tells me her younger sister was always a "twig," a gorgeous, size-0 dancer. "She was always the one people remarked on because she's so pretty and petite," she says. "She and I are close in age, so she was always there. I don't think anyone compared us in a bad way, but all the praise for one aspect makes the other aware of what she's lacking. We frequently talk about how my mother pigeonholed us and still thinks of us in certain ways, despite what else we've become. It was that comparison that really triggered a change in the way I felt about my body. I can almost recall when I figured it out. I was sitting on the school bus, and I couldn't have been more than eight. And I don't remember feeling anything but resigned to it—not sad, just accepting."

When our comments indicate to our daughters that there's power in being the pretty one, we set them up for a lifetime of comparing, measuring, and focusing on the ways that they aren't good enough. "You know that 'we all come in different shapes and sizes' talk?" says Susan. "It's true, but it's hard to believe when the person next to you has a much more desirable shape and size."

As moms, the words we use to talk to our girls about other women's bodies also can have a deep and lasting effect on the way they feel about themselves. Constantly praising one daughter's shapely legs—and saying nothing to the other—is bound to leave one daughter feeling pretty and powerful and the other feeling—well, not. A friend of mine tells me that the mother of one of her daughter's friends likes to let my friend's daughter borrow clothes and often compliments her on her appearance. I can't help but wonder how that makes her own daughter feel, hearing her mom heap praise on another girl's looks.

I can remember once feeling incredibly jealous of a distant cousin I'd never even met. When my parents returned from a visit, my mother went on and on about how beautiful this "tall, California blonde" cousin was. I tried to be the mature adult I was supposed to be (I was in my early twenties at the time), but inside I was seething. Let's just say that my mother's out-of-character, over-the-top praise of this cousin's beauty—which, from her description, was everything that I wasn't—infuriated my envious inner child. A year later, knowing I'd get a chance to meet her at a family wedding, I was resigned to sitting next to a Christie Brinkley look-alike. Imagine my shock when in walked a pretty but still fairly average-looking girl.

You may be thinking that girls should be able to tolerate hearing their moms compliment someone else—after all, the world doesn't revolve around them, and our admiration of another girl's beauty or accomplishments or personality doesn't take anything away from the love we have for our daughters. That's true, but it's also a very adult way of thinking, and adolescents may not quite be there yet. If you want to know (sort of) how it feels, close your eyes, and imagine your husband or significant other repeatedly complimenting and admiring another woman who looks very different from the way you look. You'd have to be incredibly secure for it not to bother you after a while. And adolescents aren't exactly known for being secure in themselves.

You've Got Your Mother's Thighs

Growing up, as I listened to my mother point out her body's flaws to anyone who'd listen, I filed two facts away: One, it was normal to not like your body. Two, if I had a stomach, thighs, upper arms—you name it—like my mother's, my body must not be good enough. After all, that's what she'd been telling me for years. Not through her comments about my body, of course, but through her comments about her own.

Most of us would never say those kinds of things to our daughters about their bodies. We'd probably never make those comments to our friends, either. Yet we have no problem pointing out and talking at length about our fat butts, jiggling thighs, flat chests, skinny chicken legs, or flabby upper arms. It's as if we're drawing a road map to self-hatred for our girls.

The reality is this: Speaking positively about ourselves in front of our daughters is one of the greatest gifts we can give them. Not only does it teach them to think outside the language of self-criticism that's all too common among girls and women, it also spares them from having to draw the logical conclusion that they're unattractive when their bodies develop the very shape we've been criticizing in our own for years. After all, you can't get away with telling a girl that her legs are just fine if they're shaped like yours and you've been calling yours "skinny chicken legs" for years. She's way too smart for that.

Maura has taken full advantage of her twelve-year-old daughter's budding reasoning skills when trying to help her feel good about her body. Maura lost about twenty-five pounds a couple of years ago, and says she and her daughter can now share clothes. "She was very conscious of my weight loss, and she'd say, 'Wow, Mom, you look so good,'" Maura tells me. "Every once in a while now, she'll say something like, 'Mom, do you think I'm fat?' It doesn't happen very often, but when it does, I'll say, 'You always tell me how great I look. We wear the same size, so how could you be fat? How can you say that Mom looks great but you're fat, when we wear the same size?' And she'll say, 'Oh, OK.' It's logic."

Sometimes, all we want is validation, whether it's from our moms, our friends, or the world at large. Let's be honest: Who doesn't like to be told that they look great? I certainly enjoyed it during my year with *Shape*. In fact, it was hard to get used to not being told how great I was looking once the weight had finally come off.

Maura's in touch with that feeling. At first, she says, she enjoyed the compliments and accolades while she was losing weight. "Eventually, though, people stop saying it because you haven't changed, and that would really bother me," she says. "I'd be like, 'Do I not look good anymore?' So now I try to recognize that it's not all about the compliments. It's about being healthy and feeling good and not putting so much emphasis on what other people think of me."

Our concern—or lack thereof—for what others think about the way we look is also shaping how our girls feel about their bodies. If we're constantly worried about how we measure up to the other women in our lives, or if we're constantly seeking reassurance through compliments or by dressing to ensure that all eyes are on us when we walk into a room, we're sending our girls a strong message. We're teaching them that appearance is a way to feel "greater than" or "less than" another woman.

"My mom would always compare herself to others—even our family and friends," Melanie, age twenty-four, tells me. "We had a family friend, and my mom would always ask, 'Am I bigger than her? Am I smaller?' It's funny, but I used to do that to my sisters on the beach. I'd be like, 'See that girl? Do I look like her? Am I bigger than her or smaller?' And my sister said, 'Oh my God. You're just like Mom.'"

As Melanie's story shows, our daughters are quick to pick up the words we use to talk about ourselves, as well as the ways we behave toward our bodies—whether they're conscious of it or not. That's why it's so important to stop and think about what we're saying before the words escape our lips.

"The words we use are really important," says Amber Rickert, MSW, MPH, a clinical social worker who works with adolescents at a residential facility. "I know from being a mother that my child remembers everything that comes out of my mouth. And as a therapist, I know that how I frame things is very important when I talk to my kids."

Still, Rickert says it's OK to talk about the complexities of body image with your daughter. We just have to be careful of what we say and how we say it. It's much better to say, "I'm PMSing right now, so I'm not feeling very good about my body today," than it is to simply launch into a litany of your body's faults. Doing that also sends girls the important message that just because we feel one way about our bodies today, it doesn't mean we'll feel that way forever. That's a pretty powerful concept during a time when girls' bodies are changing rapidly.

Figuring Out the Right Thing to Say

So what do you say when your daughter comes to you and says, "Mom, am I fat?"

It's a pivotal moment, isn't it?

Chances are, you won't always find the right thing to say to your daughter, but you can try. Abby says that when her daughter, Tammy, complains about her body, she'll take a moment to evaluate the situation and try to get to the root of what's really bothering her. Did somebody make a comment? Did a new outfit not fit the way she wanted it to? Could it be hormonal? Ultimately, though, she tries to always tell Tammy the truth.

"I think she doesn't want to be bullshitted," she says. "She doesn't want me to say, 'But you're beautiful.' I respect her enough not to do that. So that's when I'll say, 'Well, what do you want to do? Do you want to get more active? Do you want to start eating a little bit more healthy?' I think the best thing I can do for her really is to give her some sort of plan of attack."

We all know that with adolescents, it's best not to offer comments, suggestions, or critiques unless they ask for it, and even then, we best tread carefully. But if she comes to you, Rickert says, sometimes the best thing to do is remind her that when it comes to her body, she's not yet looking at a finished product.

"You can remind her that her body's changing and she's got to hang in there," she says. That's also good advice for moms who are going through body changes of their own. Our bodies—and how we feel about them— are constantly evolving. So when it comes to the words we choose to use, don't say something in front of your daughter today that you'll regret tomorrow.

Body Image Builders

Moms are powerful. What we say about our bodies—and those of our daughters—has a lasting effect on the way they see themselves. Not sure how to handle those tricky body moments that sometimes crop up? Here's some advice:

Watch your words. Sure, sometimes it's tempting to let loose with a wisecrack or a disparaging comment about your body when you look in the mirror. But if your daughter's in the room, think of her, and bite your tongue.

Question her questions. If she asks your opinion—"Are my legs fat?" "Do these pants make my butt look big?"—turn it around, and ask her what she thinks. By probing a little, you may be able to find out what she needs to hear.

Try a little time-travel. Before you unleash a criticism of what she's wearing or even the slightest comment about her body, stop, close your eyes, and remember what it was like to be an adolescent. Remind yourself of how you felt when your mom spoke to you about your body, and let that be your guide.

Spread it around. It's OK to praise your daughter's appearance from time to time, and to praise the appearance of other girls. Just remember to dole it out fairly and not make your praise about appearance all the time for any one person.

Mind your mannerisms. Remember that looks, gestures, and sighs can hurt just as much as words.

The X(Y) Factor:
Boys, Brothers, Dads,
and Husbands

The Male Influence on Body Feelings

> One of my friends has hinted that I don't have a
> boyfriend because of the way I look. She said,
> "You're really cute and all, but boys want more
> than that. You should try makeup and tighter
> clothes."
>
> —*Katherine, age fourteen*

Faith was ten the first time a boy made her feel bad about her body. It was spring, and she was wearing shorts on one of the first warm days of the season. She was sitting on the school bus, chatting happily with her friends, when all of a sudden a boy in her class—whom she'd liked very much up until then—leaned over the seat and said, "Hey, your legs are hairy."

She got off the bus that afternoon visibly upset. When I asked her what was wrong, she told me what he'd said. "Of course your legs have hair—you're ten," was what I wanted to say. Instead, I believe I said something mature and along the lines of, "He's a jerk. Just ignore him."

But she couldn't ignore him. Later that night, she came to me and said, "Mom, can I shave my legs?"

Caught off guard I said, "Let me think about it."

And I did think about it—for days. I so wanted to tell her that she was perfect the way she was. I wanted to tell her that she didn't have to change something about herself just because some silly boy said something unkind. I thought maybe it would just blow over, until I noticed she wore long pants every day after that. I couldn't believe the inner turmoil I was feeling; on the one hand, she was only ten. This was just the beginning of her having to face judgments and criticism from the outside world, and I didn't want her to think that changing her appearance was the right way to deal with other people's "issues." But on the other hand, it was only hair. If it was making her feel so self-conscious that she refused to wear shorts, then why shouldn't I let her shave it?

I can remember sitting on the edge of my bed, asking myself what my mother would have done in this situation. Ultimately, I knew: She'd have told me to let her shave.

So I called Faith into my room, and I said, "You know, if you really want to shave your legs because *you* want to, then I'll let you. But I hope you're not doing this just because some boy said you should."

"I really want to, Mom," she said, throwing her arms around me.

The next day, I went to the drugstore and bought her an electric razor designed for girls—then promptly took it out to the car and cried right there in the Walgreens parking lot. I couldn't figure out why this was bothering me so much. It wasn't that I didn't want her to grow up; I guess I was just feeling the ground start to shift beneath my feet. She'd always been so confident and so secure, and to see her react this way to a boy's comment felt like the beginning of something that was bigger than I was—something I wasn't sure I was equipped to handle.

That night, I taught her how to shave her legs with the razor, and the next day, she proudly wore her shorts. When she got home from school, I said, "Well?"

"He said, 'Your legs are hairy,' so I picked up my leg, and I said, 'Are they?'" she said. "And he said, 'Oh.'"

The look on her face was priceless, and I was glad I had allowed her to have that moment of sweet vindication. And truthfully, she didn't pick up that razor again for almost a year.

***

It can be scary, uncomfortable, and downright thrilling for girls when boys begin to notice the way their bodies

en I was in sixth grade—long before the passage
ual harassment laws and zero-tolerance policies in
nool—bra snapping was the norm. I can also remember
getting my behind pinched quite a few times, which ap-
parently I was supposed to take as a compliment. There
was one boy in particular who would steal up behind me
in the hallway and whisper, "Nice butt," before giving it a
pinch. When I told my mother about it, she wasn't at all
horrified as I thought she would be. "I guess he likes you"
was all she said.

That was a bit confusing.

In fact, when it came to the boys, middle school was
a deliciously confusing time, as coed games of tag on the
playground soon gave way to games of spin-the-bottle in
somebody's darkened basement. By fourteen, I can remember, none of the girls in my group of friends wanted
to wear jackets—we were all too busy showing off our
new breasts. There was a certain power in knowing that
we were leaving our little-girl bodies behind—and that
the boys were looking.

But with the looking, of course, comes the judgment—
who's hot and who's not—and that feeling of being eval-
uated can be downright icky, especially as girls begin to
measure themselves against their friends. It's tough on us
moms, too. We can only watch from the sidelines as our
daughters struggle not only with their changing bodies,
but with trying to figure out what's attractive to boys, and
with what they're willing to do to get a boy's attention.

Sexuality Starts at Home

It's not nearly as creepy as it sounds. It's simply that home is where girls first learn how to relate to the opposite sex—growing up, I always felt comfortable around boys, thanks to my two older brothers. They were just fifteen months apart, and through them I learned that rough-housing, teasing, put-downs, and seemingly endless pestering were a part of how boys related to each other and to the world. At times they hurt my feelings, but from them I learned a valuable lesson: that a boy who makes fun of and teases a girl isn't always doing it because he thinks badly of her. Often, it's the opposite that's true.

Though they were close in age to each other, they were just about done with high school and pretty much past the teasing years when my body started to change—a fact for which I'm eternally grateful. But some women, like Karin, remember all too well what it was like to have brothers bear witness to their changing bodies. When she was twelve, though she was just a bit chubby, she says, one of her three brothers decided he was going to call her "porker," and the others soon followed suit.

"I can remember feeling odd then and wondering why they were calling me that," she says. "My mother told me to just ignore them—sticks and stones and all that. She said, 'Just ignore them, and they'll stop.' That was usually the answer to anything like that when you were being teased."

Ignoring doesn't always work, though—especially if the teaser can see that he's getting a reaction. And brothers can be masters of getting the reaction; in fact, when girls get teased about their appearance, it's most likely to come from their brothers, according to Dr. Andrea Vazzana of the NYU Child Study Center. And, she adds, those kinds of comments really stay with girls.

When brothers make fun of their sisters' bodies, our first instinct as moms might be that of Karin's mother: Tell her to just ignore him. Truthfully, if I felt compelled to step in to resolve every "fight" between Faith and her younger brother, I'd want to get in my car and just drive away. Sibling squabbles are almost a given, but body teasing is something different. Being teased and tormented about your physical appearance in childhood and early adolescence is often how a lifetime of body image struggles begins. Like pulling weeds from the garden, it's our job to nip that kind of meanness in the bud.

If it's going on in your house, the first thing to do is talk to your son privately. Ask him why he's teasing his sister about her body, but don't be surprised to hear that he doesn't think he's hurting her. Remember my brothers and their endless put-downs of each other? There is evidence that that kind of talk is more the norm for boys. According to "Behavior Problems: Name-Calling and Teasing: Information for Parents and Educators" from the National Association of School Psychologists, boys tend to tease about what they perceive as areas of weakness, and by the time they're in the upper-elementary and middle-school grades, their teasing is often related to an interest in girls—and a desire to hide that interest so they won't be teased themselves.[1] But boys are also unique in that they typically don't hold grudges against each other for teasing; two boys may tease each other mercilessly at recess and be best buddies again by lunch. Girls are more likely to hold on to teasing, especially when it's appearance related. Starting in the preteen years, writes Dr. Anita Gurian of the NYU Child Study Center, a girl's body becomes "an all consuming passion and barometer of worth."[2]

That's why it's so important to point out to our sons that teasing *does* hurt her and to try to get them to see it from her point of view, says Dr. Tina Tessina, a psychotherapist and author of *Money, Sex, and Kids: Stop Fighting about the Three Things that Can Ruin Your Marriage.* If you were teased by your brothers about your body when you were growing up, sharing those stories with your son—and letting him know how much they affected you and hurt you—might help him see things from his sister's perspective.

Another thing that can help is teaching your daughter to evaluate the source of the criticism—just as you did when teaching her how to deal with comments from mean girls. Teasing and criticism always have more to do with the person doing the criticizing, so encourage her to consider her brother's situation. Is he being picked on at school? Is there a girl he likes who won't give him the time of day? Is he feeling left out of the closeness she shares with you? It's a great time to remind her, too, that just because somebody says something doesn't mean it's true.

When Dads Act Dopey

Sometimes, dads play a role in making their daughters feel bad about their bodies. My own father was notorious for pointing out flaws; he didn't do it to be purposely mean—I suspect he just wasn't thinking. I remember waking up one morning when I was about fourteen and discovering that I had developed an enormous angry red pimple on my chin during the night. I tried frantically to cover it with makeup and hoped that no one would notice, but as soon as I sat down at the breakfast table, my dad looked up and said, "You know, you've got a big pimple on your chin."

Oh, really?

Those were the sort of comments that were standard in our house when I was growing up. But some girls have dads who take teasing too far; one woman I spoke to says she started feeling very self-conscious about her body when one day, her father called her "Crisco"—as in "fat in the can."

Fathers really need to be careful about what she calls "judgmental teasing," says Dr. Vazzana, recalling a former patient with an eating disorder whose father habitually called her chubby and put her on a diet. "Even years later, her memories of this are painful," she tells me. "The shame she felt really shaped how she feels about herself."

Though my husband, John, never teases Faith about her body, he's sometimes perplexed by her reaction to the little "jokes" he makes. In some ways, it's just like the boy who teases a girl because he secretly likes her. John will make a teasing comment about something Faith's wearing or the way her hair is sticking up when she first wakes up, and soon she'll be watery-eyed, leaving him looking at me, saying, "What did I say?"

I've talked to them both separately, letting him know that sometimes a "joke" feels like criticism or humiliation. With Faith, I've explained that joking and teasing are how boys and men often relate to each other, and how they show that they like someone. Dad jokes with her, I tell her, because he likes her and wants to show it. But if something he says makes her feel bad, she needs to speak up and let him know.

Jokes and innocent comments gone horribly wrong are pretty common among fathers and daughters at this age. Dads don't always get that the things they say about a girl's appearance—or about a wife's appearance, for that matter—can often come across as judgment. And because fathers are the first men in their daughters' lives, their opinions hold a lot of weight, even if daughters like to pretend that they don't.

"I remember once my sister got up from the table, and my dad said, 'You have pretty short legs, don't you?'"

fifteen-year-old Sophie tells me. "I'm sure it was just one of those 'Oh, I never realized' moments, but she was still upset. He keeps his mouth shut now. He's pretty much come to terms with the fact that he lives in a house with four women, and he's learned the hard way not to comment on what we look like."

As moms, we can help the man in our daughter's life understand that jokes and seemingly benign comments about her body or her appearance can hurt—and the hurt can last for a long time. Girls tend to take what their dads say to heart, though they may seem to just brush it off. But girls are also deeply affected by what their fathers and brothers say about the appearance of *other* girls and women. Remember: In adolescence, girls are very focused on how they compare to other girls, as well as with media images of women. When dads and brothers put another girl or woman down, joke about her appearance, or offer extensive commentary on why she's sexually attractive, our daughters are listening and silently measuring themselves against what they hear.

"My father always had a comment about everyone's weight," Maura tells me. "It was always, 'That one's put on a lot of weight' or 'She needs to cut back.' He recently told me that I was getting too skinny and that I didn't look like a girl anymore. I can't win; either it's too much, or I'm too little. It's never just right. I can laugh that off now at thirty-seven, but I couldn't do it at fifteen."

The bottom line, says Dr. Tessina, is that if you hear your son or your husband teasing your daughter about her body or her weight—or if she comes to you and tells you it's happening—you absolutely have to step in. "Talk to Dad in private," she says. "Let him know that [teasing] is not acceptable, even if his parents did it to him. Mom really has to put her foot down. And above all, don't be critical yourself. You're the role model."

Don't forget, too, that just as your daughter is watching how you treat your body and what you say about it, she's also watching what her dad says and does, too—about your body and his own.

"I was more influenced by my father than my mother when it came to my body," says Sarah Maria, age twenty-nine, a body image coach who once struggled with an eating disorder and now runs Break Free Beauty, a company dedicated to helping people love their bodies and themselves. "My mom always exercised when I was growing up and kept herself physically fit. She didn't have issues with her body and was pretty down to earth about the whole thing. But my father struggled incessantly with his own weight. He would overeat and then not eat, or overeat and then say, 'I need to exercise to go burn the weight.' It's a struggle for him; there's no peace to it. I was very influenced by that."

When she lost a lot of weight and was below a hundred pounds, her father praised her and told her she looked great. Because her father was always struggling to control his own weight, she says, controlling her weight became a way for her to please her father.

It's important that we recognize the influence that fathers and brothers have on our girls. Dads who openly ogle rail-thin women with big breasts in front of their daughters are sending them a not-so-subtle message about what's required to be attractive to men. Brothers who feel free to "critique" the appearance of every girl—or who are allowed to make derogatory comments about women and their appearance—are teaching their sisters that their bodies are subject to boys' evaluation and that they'd better look a certain way to be pleasing to them. The men in our lives sometimes need to be reminded that their words, actions, and attitudes have a lasting impact on the girls in their lives.

Crushed by a Crush

"A guy that I like has said that I was hot to some of his friends."—Kayla, age twelve

"Boys are stupid, for the most part. . . . I usually end up adoring guys way out of my league. Sometimes, they call me fat, and I don't really care. That's what they think, and I don't have to agree. But in sixth grade we got spring pictures, and one of my close guy friends at the time came up to me and said, 'Your picture came out really nice. You look really pretty.' It was so sweet."
—Amanda, age thirteen

"I have a really tiny build, but long legs and pretty large boobs. For some reason, that combination tends to attract a lot of stares, and that can definitely get annoying—especially when guys talk to your boobs instead of your face. On the other hand, it's nice to be noticed when it's by someone who can appreciate them on top of my sense of humor and other important things."—Sophie, age fifteen

Of course, adolescence is about discovering your place in the world outside your family, and boys are very much a part of that world for our daughters. Remember your first crush? If he liked you back or thought you were cute, you were walking on air. But if he didn't—devastation doesn't quite cover it, does it?

I had a crush on a boy a year ahead of me in middle school. Somehow, it got back to him that I liked him, but he didn't know who I was. I happened to be in the cafeteria one day when he walked in with a couple of his buddies. One of them pointed at me and said, "There she is." He took one look at me and said, "*That's* her?" Let's just say his tone of voice wasn't exactly complimentary.

Like I said: devastation.

Girls—and their body image—are particularly vulnerable when they enter the world of boy-girl relationships. A word or a look from a boyfriend can trigger a body image crisis and then some. What did he mean by that? Am I not pretty enough? Am I fat?

Lisa tells me she began to doubt her body after a boyfriend wondered why her hips and thighs weren't as skinny as the rest of her. "I had never thought of myself as anything other than thin and in shape," she says. "But when he said that, I was more aware of my hips and thighs and more self-conscious, especially in a bikini."

Pam, now forty-five and the mother of a twelve-year-old daughter, shares a similar story. She tells me she was thin and healthy at fourteen but started to second-guess her body when her boyfriend at the time painted a picture of her that he thought was fabulous. "The girl in the picture had a big butt," she says. "I didn't think my butt was big before I saw that picture. Eventually, I just decided to believe he was a lousy artist."

Pam's decision to attribute the big-butted picture to her boyfriend's lousy painting skills is actually a great example of how to handle body criticisms. Teaching our daughters to look at *who* is doing the criticizing and *what* might be motivating it keeps them from internalizing a boy's harsh words and believing that they're true. Boys who are pushing for more sexual activity than a girl might be comfortable with have also been known to tell her she's fat or ugly or otherwise unlovable.

Because our girls are not only listening to what we say but also watching our behavior, we have to remember that how we relate to the men in our lives is teaching them how to relate to boys.

Pam says her husband often blurts out whatever he thinks and has sometimes made comments about her body that made her feel self-conscious. "He'll tell me that I dress too old or that I should wear earrings and makeup all the time," she says. "He sees me as his reflection to the world. I used to believe him and try to please him, but it's not possible, so I don't try anymore. Only he can make himself happy. But I do worry about how he affects our daughter's body image."

Even if we think they're not paying attention, our girls are always watching what we're willing to accept from the men in our circle. If your husband tells you that you don't look good in that dress—the dress you bought when she was with you and she knows you love—do you run upstairs and change it? Or do you tell him, "Really? I love this dress," and wear it confidently? If he wonders aloud if you've put on a few pounds recently, will she see you eating only salad and heading out for an extra-long run the next day? Or will she hear you tell him, "Nope, I'm just fine. Besides, I feel great," as you prepare a healthy meal for the family? Either response sends her a message about her body and her body image—and the power men will or won't have over it.

So what can you do when she comes to you saying that a boy has made fun of her physical attributes? First, gently determine how she feels about what he's said. Does his opinion matter to her? Does she agree with him? Is it something (like leg shaving) she can easily change and that *she* wants to change? It's not necessarily bad to make changes, even if the idea arose in response to teasing—as long as the change is *her* idea, says Dr. Tessina. But teach her to always evaluate the criticism—and its source—before she decides to make a change, she says. One of the best ways to do that is to examine our own response to criticism, "jokes," and other comments from the men we know. If our girls see us stand up for ourselves or simply brush off a man's stupid comment without feeling that we need to change ourselves to meet someone else's idea of attractiveness, they'll be much more likely to do the same.

We can also help our girls bolster their body image as they enter the world of boys by showing them that romantic relationships aren't only about physical attractiveness. Boys and men will always look at pretty girls and women, but you can help your daughter see that other qualities, like being smart, caring, and funny, can be just as attractive, so it's better to spend time developing those qualities than obsessing over real or imagined body flaws. And if she is physically attractive to boys, it's even more important to teach her to value herself for something other than her looks.

Melissa, age twenty-eight, remembers once being asked out and turning the guy down because his previous girlfriend was really pretty.

"In high school, and even through college, I never had a shapely body. I was a late bloomer," she says. "And I was always like, 'What guy is going to want me?' especially if he had dated someone who was really pretty or voluptuous. I made some kind of excuse and avoided dating him. I look back now, and I wish I never did anything like that. But you live and learn."

Body Image Builders

Males, whether boys at school, brothers at home, dads, or other relatives, can have a big effect on a girl's body image. But you can help your daughter learn to keep teasing and other odd boy behavior in perspective. Here's how:

Monitor sibling squabbles. If the fighting progresses to teasing about weight, their bodies, or other physical attributes—on either side—step in, and stop it in its tracks. Help them both understand that damaging and hurtful comments can't be unsaid.

Share your stories. Help your son or husband understand how hurtful teasing and comments about her body can be by sharing stories from your own body image past. Make sure they know that childhood nicknames and other body comments can stick with us—and affect us—into adulthood.

Be aware of "boy troubles." Talk to your daughter about your own adolescent relationships, and make sure she knows that boys don't always say what they mean, especially when they're in front of their friends or trying to get a girl's attention.

Have the big talk. You know the one I'm talking about. But she needs more than just an explanation of mechanics. It's time for a talk about respecting our bodies and the psychological effects of becoming sexually active. Make sure she knows that although sexual activity might seem like a one-way ticket to popularity with the boys, it can ultimately lead to rejection and feeling pretty awful about yourself.

Don't freak out. As boys become important to her and her friends, you may see and hear things that make you want to stand up and scream. Don't. Do everything you can to keep her talking to you so that you'll have opportunities to gently remind her of your family's values and of the importance of respecting herself and her body above all else.

Success Is for Skinny Girls

How Body Image Affects Confidence

*A pretty girl is attractive, smart, funny, and kind.
If I had a friend who didn't like her body, I would
tell her that it's what's on the inside that counts.*

—Kayla, age twelve

It was a Tuesday night, and a hush fell over the gymnasium as Faith stepped forward to the microphone. The pale blue earrings she'd chosen to compliment her blue-striped shirt jingled ever so slightly as she tilted her head and considered the word the caller had just said. This was it—the townwide spelling bee—and the winner here would determine who would represent the school at the state bee and, quite possibly, the national bee in Washington, DC.

Pretty high stakes for a sixth grader.

Some of the other competitors had whispered and stammered and stared at their feet when it was their turn at the mike, but not my girl. She took a deep breath, spelled the word confidently, and grinned from ear to ear when the judge pronounced her correct.

Faith has always loved being center stage. Whether it was a dance recital, a band concert, an outing on the pitcher's mound, or a solo sung in church, her confidence has never failed to amaze me. As for her appearance, she'd always been content to wear whatever I suggested, but that's changing. She takes pride in putting her own fashion stamp on what she wears now, and lately I've noticed her struggling with choosing an outfit when she knows she has to get up in front of people. Just recently, she tried on at least seven outfits, trying to decide what to wear for a music festival performance, before settling on a skirt, tank top, and crocheted jacket. Earrings were changed multiple times, and although she asked my opinion, I could tell she didn't really want honesty. What she wanted most was for me to agree with her choice.

Sigh . . . Things sure are changing around here. My girl is growing up.

She's her own person now, and she wants the world to know it. These days, her friends' opinions matter more than—or at least just as much as—mine do. Part of me is thrilled to watch her transform from a little girl into an accomplished young woman. But part of me is also sad to see her leave the carefree days of little girlhood behind. She's more focused on what others think of her now. I know it's normal adolescent behavior. In fact, teenagers are notorious for their egocentric worldview; they think it's all about them, and they can't imagine that maybe other people are thinking about their own concerns. Girls at this age are sure that everybody is looking at them, judging them, and potentially finding them lacking.

I know the time is coming when Faith may be more concerned about what she looks like than whether she spells a word correctly. The time may also come when she's so concerned with what others think that she'll no longer get up to take her place at center stage. I'm ashamed to admit that I've been there. At times in my life, the fear of being judged as fat or ugly or otherwise unworthy has kept me from raising my hand, standing up to speak, or taking full advantage of personal and professional opportunities that have come my way.

As a young magazine editor, I was once asked to speak at a trade association meeting. It was a great chance to practice my public speaking skills and to generate publicity for the magazine. But as I stood at the podium that day, I didn't feel like the confident expert the audience likely saw. Instead, I remember feeling frumpy in the blue suit I'd chosen to wear—it didn't fit quite right, and it wasn't the most flattering look on my frame. I remember hoping that the podium was hiding enough of me. Throughout that speech, my cheeks felt as if they were on fire, and I just wanted the whole ordeal to end.

Sometimes, when I watch Faith performing in public, the memories of that speaking engagement come flooding back to me. Had I really been so distracted by what I looked like that day that I failed to take full advantage of the terrific career-building moment right in front of me? It's a memory that makes me sad—and furious!

Still, when I agreed to write the Weight-Loss Diary, being judged was my biggest fear. Putting a number to my weight, admitting that I found myself lacking in some way, and shining a light on all the bad habits that had led me to this point took me way past uncomfortable. But, I knew that if I could do this—if I could face down my "flaws" and confront my bad body image, what I perceived to be the biggest thing that held me back— the outcome would be no less than life-changing. In fact, Pavitra Ciavardone, my life coach on the project, hit the nail right on the head when about six weeks into our work together she said, "This is about so much more than twenty-five pounds, isn't it?"

Indeed.

Growing up, the message—through words and behavior—was always that you can be smart, funny, kind, caring, a productive employee, a good friend, a loving wife, and a terrific mother, but if you're overweight, you're flawed. You're not the complete package. But the bigger message was that the flaws in our bodies could be seen by others, and it was our responsibility to protect other people from having to look at those flaws. No wearing a bathing suit at the beach (it might, *gasp*, subject other beachgoers to our flabby thighs or spider vein–covered legs). No raising your hand to speak (people would *look* at you). And definitely no calling attention to yourself (people would wonder just who you *thought* you were). The message I got, loud and clear, was that being judged by others—and failing to measure up—was intolerable and should be avoided at all costs.

Judging Ourselves

Though worrying about measuring up to our peers is rampant during adolescence, plenty of moms struggle with how they compare to their peer group as well. Moms have been known to jealously whisper to each other about other women who seem to have it all together— great marriage, great house, great kids, and maybe a great career, too. And if she's also physically attractive? Well, that seems like the biggest "sin" of all, doesn't it? In truth, nobody likes to feel judged, and the people who claim not to care at all what other people think of them are probably lying.

Make no mistake—our girls are listening to, and are affected by, the ways in which we feel we measure up— or don't—to other women. Whether we make cutting comments about someone else or point ourselves out as lacking in comparison, girls learn to judge themselves— and each other—harshly through our example. When we hold ourselves to unrealistic standards or imply that our accomplishments don't matter as much as any extra pounds we may be carrying or as much as some other real or imagined body flaw, we teach our daughters that for women, "success," in the end, boils down to what you look like.

That's a dangerous message to send, says Polly Young-Eisendrath, PhD, an analyst and author of *The Self-Esteem Trap: Raising Confident and Compassionate Kids in an Age of Self-Importance*, who has also run groups for women with eating disorders.

"There's a whole world of stuff all tangled up around a woman's appearance," she says. "Mothers teach their daughters that appearance is a certain kind of power, and the issue of appearance always trumps a woman's accomplishments."

I know just what Dr. Young-Eisendrath means. It's what drives women to starvation diets in an effort to lose weight before a class reunion. So what if you've become a doctor, a lawyer, a teacher, or a mother of six terrific kids—if you've gained weight since high school or college, you're worried that that's how you'll be judged by your former classmates. They won't remember your hard work or your accomplishments, you fear; they'll remember only your pudge.

But how we feel about the way we look affects more than just the big milestone events in our lives. It also affects the things we do, or don't do, on a day-to-day basis. Karin, mom to a thirteen-year-old daughter, confesses that she's stayed home when friends wanted to go out because she didn't feel good about her body that day.

"I remember just feeling 'blech' about my weight and appearance," she says. "And I didn't want to go out with these skinny girls who are going to go out on the dance floor, and I just feel like two-ton. . . . My friend and I went out with another friend one time, and I remember noticing that their hair was long and styled, and I'd just chopped my hair off. My friend is also pretty thin, and I was struggling with my weight again. I was envious. I was sitting on the other side of the table from them, and I was thinking, 'Oh, there's definitely a line drawn here.'"

Kind of sad, isn't it? But we've all been there at some point—in that place where we're so caught up in feeling bad about ourselves that we can't enjoy the moment we're in right now. Here's a prime example: When I look at photographs from a Disney World vacation we took when my kids were much younger, I recognize the all-too-familiar expression on my face. The smile is there, but the eyes are saying, "Please don't take my picture." Instead of enjoying a magical moment with my babies, I'm pretty sure I was thinking about how fat I was going to look in the photo.

Maura, mom to two girls, says she didn't even want to keep the pictures from the christening of one of her daughters because she hated the way she looked. She stuck them in a drawer, she says, and even now that she's lost weight, it's still tough to look at them. "It was really hard to be that unhappy with how I looked," she says, admitting that when she was at her heaviest, she'd often duck into a store if she spotted someone she hadn't seen in a while at the mall. "I remember seeing someone I went to high school with, and I was just mortified. I remember thinking, 'I cannot possibly talk to that person. I don't want them to see me looking like this.'"

Think about how that kind of behavior affects our daughters. I'll confess I've turned my head away when I was at my heaviest and saw someone I knew in public, hoping they didn't see me first and that they wouldn't recognize me. But in doing that, I know I must have given Faith a skewed idea of how important appearance is—not to mention teaching her that other people's judgments mattered so much that I had to hide.

A Life Beyond Your Body

Moms need to be careful that they don't give their daughters the impression that success in life all comes down to how much you weigh, says Dr. Young-Eisendrath.

"Whatever your appearance is, you have to get comfortable with it," she says. "And you have to be engaged with something in your life beyond your body and your home that's meaningful to you. If a mom can show by example that there's a great big world out there and it really has little to do with appearance, that will come back to her girl."

Engaging in a meaningful activity, whether it's education, politics, career, or activism, is exactly why how we feel about our bodies—and the example we set for our daughters—is so important. I don't mean to sound overly dramatic, but how we feel about the way we look affects the ultimate trajectory of our lives. The young girl who never offers her opinion in class because she doesn't want everyone to turn and look at her, seeing how "wrong" she looks in the outfit she chose that day, may never build the confidence she'll need as a doctor diagnosing a patient's illness. The professional woman who turns down an opportunity to speak at a conference because she's "too fat" to get up in front of all those colleagues may never get the promotion that will take her beyond an assistant's role. And consider the more subtle impact of the millions of women of all ages who appear to have it all together, but inside spend countless hours thinking about the ways their bodies don't measure up to an ideal. Imagine what could have been accomplished with that time and energy.

Abby's story is a classic example of how body image affects confidence. After losing twenty-six pounds at the age of almost forty, she says she definitely noticed a difference in her daily life. But it wasn't so much that other people were treating her differently—it was that *she* was perceiving things differently.

"I'd act more outgoing, so other people were more outgoing, too," she says. "I was more apt to have a conversation with someone. I'm an outgoing person anyway, but I felt more confident. I was taking grad classes, and although I knew my stuff, I didn't feel insecure about speaking anymore because I felt like I had the look to go along with the knowledge. When I feel chubby, I'll let someone else do the talking. It's sad, but it's true."

Cindy, who is thirty-seven and has struggled with her weight all her life, agrees with Abby and says that how she looks has affected so much of her behavior—and what she's believed she could do. She's so uncomfortable with her appearance sometimes that she's often "anxious" about how others will judge her. "I strive to be extra helpful, extra articulate, extra right when someone's asking me something so that they can find something else worthy about me," she tells me. "One thing my mother did make perfectly clear was that the world finds it unacceptable to be overweight."

That's a legacy Cindy is desperately trying to change for her own daughter.

"I want my daughter to know that what *she* thinks matters," she says. "I know that what everyone else thinks always plays in, but I want her to believe her own opinion. I want her to know that if you feel like you look good when you leave the house, then you look good when you leave the house."

"Act As If"

So much of body image is about what we *tell* ourselves about our bodies. When we leave the house feeling self-conscious and down about the way we look, that feeling affects just about everything we do that day. But just as we need to remind our daughters that everybody has something she'd like to change about herself, we need to remind ourselves, too. Sometimes all it takes is a shift in perspective: Sure, you may think that skinny mom at the bus stop is so lucky because she always looks great in whatever she's wearing, but maybe she's thin from not eating because she's too busy worrying about a sick parent.

I bumped into a woman recently who'd heard that I was writing this book. She put her hand on my arm and said, "You know, I spent my whole life thinking that tall, thin blondes have it made. But then God sent me my daughter, who's a tall, thin blonde, and I realize now that they feel just as insecure as the rest of us."

I can remember my mother once telling me a story about her college years. She was so self-conscious, she said, that she used to put on her winter coat before she'd walk across the student dining hall to get her meal, so that no one could see her body underneath. When she confessed this to my grandmother, she reportedly told my mother, "What makes you think you're so important that everyone would be looking at you?"

On the one hand, ouch! But on the other hand, I've grown to see the wisdom in my grandmother's harsh words. Though I'll never know what her true motivation was, I choose to believe that she was simply trying to tell my mother that most of us are so busy thinking about our own flaws that we barely have the time or energy to notice those of other people.

It's a lesson I'm trying to teach Faith—not that she isn't important, of course, but that she isn't unique in worrying about what other people think. Knowing that other girls are just as busy fretting over what *they're* wearing and how they measure up takes some of the pressure off. But there's a bigger irony at play: Have you ever noticed that we're most attractive to other people when we forget to worry about how we look or how they're perceiving us?

When I was in the eighth grade, there was a dance at a local hall on a Saturday night, and all the kids from school were going. I'd been feeling bad about the fact that I didn't have a boyfriend when most of my friends did, and I blamed my body for it. As I got ready, I remember staring into the mirror, furiously trying to see exactly how big my butt looked in the jeans I was wearing. I was near tears; my watery eyes wreaked havoc on the mascara I'd so carefully applied.

When my friends came to get me and we walked the few blocks to the hall, something happened—something I can only describe as an "oh, screw it" feeling. At fourteen, I was already tired of hating my body and feeling bad about the way I looked. By the time we got there, I was in a great mood. I laughed, I danced, and I flirted openly with several of the boys, but what I didn't do once was think about the size of my behind. Instead of focusing on me and my flaws, I spent the entire night focused on talking to others and on what a good time I was having. By the time the dance was over, two boys had asked me out, and a third had asked for my number.

It was what Oprah would call an "aha" moment. The size of my behind certainly hadn't changed, but my attitude had.

Nancy, age forty-one, knows a bit about the concept of "act as if." Overweight all her life, Nancy spent years feeling bad about herself and, as she tells it, holding herself back. After losing some weight on a diet program and temporarily moving to a new town, she decided to try an experiment: She pretended that she was one of the prettiest, most popular girls in high school—and she acted that way.

"Even though I didn't believe I was all that, I was going to pretend that I did," she tells me. "It was completely safe because I was away from anyone I ever knew and I'd never see those people again if it didn't work. But it worked, and a lightbulb went on. And in that moment, I realized, 'You know what? There's nothing wrong with me.' It was a huge turning point."

"Acting as if" is sort of like taking my mother's mantra—if you think you're fat, you are—and flipping it on its head: If you think you're just fine, you are. It's a similar effect, I think, to that noted in a 2003 Harvard Business School study published in the *Journal of Organizational Behavior*, which found that workers who smiled felt happier at work—even if they were faking it.[1]

No one feels totally confident all the time. But if we're able to start with a baseline acceptance of who we are and what we look like, and to tell ourselves that we look good today, we can do wonders not only for our own body image, but also for our daughters' body image. As their bodies begin to change and maybe look more like our own, I can't think of a better confidence booster than having a mom who's generally happy with the way she looks.

Once we've told ourselves we look just fine, though, the key to "acting as if" is to then forget about what we look like. Think about having a photograph taken. When you're posing and you know the camera is about to flash, you tense up, acutely aware of the attention focused on you and maybe even worried about how the photo will come out. Now compare that to a lovely candid photograph snapped by a friend during a moment when you're totally relaxed and happy and not thinking about what you look like or about being photographed. It's a totally different attitude.

Body confidence is like that. It's not about perfection or even about hiding flaws. It's about Nancy's attitude of "There's nothing wrong with me." It's about saying to the world, "This is who I am."

That was what I hoped to get out of the Weight-Loss Diary experience. As I wrote in my very first column, my goal was to teach my kids that as long as you do the best you can with what you've got, there's no reason to be down on yourself. I wanted Faith to see that by exercising and eating right, I could be healthy, and my body could look the best that it possibly could. What is there to feel bad about at that point?

The nice thing about confidence is that it feeds on itself. You can start out faking it, as I did at that dance so long ago, and before you know it, it becomes genuine. Pam, age forty-five, tells me she didn't go swimming for years because she didn't want to be seen in a bathing suit. One hot day, she says, she decided she just wanted to go swimming, regardless of whether she was being judged. And guess what? The world didn't end. She went swimming and had a great time. Now, she says, she swims all the time.

Pam's setting a great example for her twelve-year-old daughter by shaking off her insecurities and diving into the pool. When our girls see us laughing, talking, swimming, connecting with others, and enjoying ourselves in the bodies we have—just as they are—we're showing them that life is about so much more than appearance.

"Confidence in yourself is way more attractive than looks," Pam says. "People are attracted to those who make *them* feel better, not to someone who's unsure and feels unworthy."

So how can we help our girls on the road to feeling confident?

Susan, age forty-four, encourages her daughters to dress well for the bodies they have.

"The right clothes make you stand taller and straighter, and you smile more because you're less worried," she says. "I call them power clothes because they give you power over your insecurities."

Abby tells me that she likes to focus on "plugging up the holes" in her daughter Tammy's self-confidence. If Tammy complains about having big feet, Abby helps her choose a beautiful pair of shoes. If she needs a new outfit, Abby says, "I'll take the time to drive her and make sure that she's comfortable and that everything fits her nice."

For Pam, helping her daughter feel more self-confident is all about being a good role model. "It must be working because she told me not to get laser surgery on my eyes, that I look good in glasses," she says. "And she tells me to let my roots and hair just be. Really, though, confidence is a battle. Nobody feels like they're the popular one, not even the popular girls. They all worry their friends will drop them, so they're afraid to just be themselves."

When we show our girls that we're fine with being ourselves—and we live our lives fully, confident in the image we present to the world—we're teaching them that the shape of our body is not the measure of our success. And if you don't feel that confidence? Act as if, and you just soon might. I promise she'll thank you for it.

Body Image Builders

Practice makes perfect, and that's true of body confidence, too. You can help your daughter feel great about the way she looks by modeling positive body feelings with these tactics:

Acknowledge her feelings. Let her know that she can come to you and vent her concerns about her body. Make sure she knows it's normal to feel down sometimes, and that everybody—even the most beautiful celebrity or the most popular girl at school—has things about herself she'd like to change.

Model confidence. Remember that confidence builds on itself. Be bold when you need to, and show her that it's good to speak your mind, take your place, and be noticed.

Mind your example. Don't refuse to wear a bathing suit or dance at a wedding because you think you're too big or don't look right. You'll be teaching her that only "perfect" people get to have fun in life.

Don't fuss—forget it. Do what you can to look your best; then forget it. Help her learn to make the most of the body she has with well-fitting clothes so she can be sure she looks her best.

PART 4

Full Circle

When Body Image Goes All Wrong

Protecting Our Girls from Eating Disorders

> I hate it when my mom says I'm thin. I wish she
> knew how fat I believe I am. I also wish my mom
> knew that I sometimes don't eat barely any
> lunch.
>
> —*Laurie, age ten*

Losing twenty-six pounds in the course of my *Shape* year—and going from a size 12 to a size 4—was definitely a dramatic body change for me. Yet it was also a slow and healthy weight loss, the result of regular cardio and strength-training workouts, better food choices, and addressing the emotional issues that triggered my overeating. But the *Shape* project wasn't my first experience with dramatic weight loss. I'd done it once before—and it was anything but healthy.

It was the summer between ninth and tenth grade. At fifteen, I was four-foot-ten, 135 pounds, and wore a size 10. I hated everything about the way I looked, but, really, I wasn't sure what to do about it. I wanted to lose weight, but I didn't know how. I wasn't in charge of meal planning, grocery shopping, or much of my own time. I remember feeling mostly sad—and fat.

The weight loss started innocently enough.

It was a blazing hot July day, and my mother had the day off, so she took my friend and me to the beach. As a treat, she bought us a bag of clam cakes from a local waterfront restaurant. We ate the hot, greasy fried treat in the heat of the sun, and as the afternoon wore on, I felt increasingly nauseated. I skipped dinner that night and breakfast the next morning, too. Every time I thought about those clam cakes, I felt ill and couldn't eat.

It was a memory I'd come to call on time and time again.

In those days, I was still stepping on the scale daily, so naturally, after a few days of very limited calories, the needle moved down a couple of pounds. I remember that moment where it suddenly clicked for me: *Hey, this is easy.*

All I had to do was not eat—a simple and reasonable solution in my fifteen-year-old mind.

By the time school started about eight weeks later— my first year of high school, which started in tenth grade where I lived—my mother had to take in all the clothes we'd bought during a mid-summer shopping trip. "Wow," she said. "You've really lost some weight."

When I stepped on the scale before going to school, the needle stopped at 102 pounds. I couldn't believe how easy it was—not only to lose the weight, but also to fool my mother into thinking I was eating. She worked all day, so I was on my own until she got home. When dinner was served, I'd take a few bites, push the food around on my plate, and tell her I'd had a big lunch. She never said much to me about it, but I knew she was thrilled with my weight loss. I loved high school in my new body, and she knew how happy I was. I made the cheerleading squad, did well in my classes, and before long I was dating a junior—an idyllic high school experience by most accounts.

It was all well and good until I had to go to her one night and tell her that I hadn't gotten my period in four months. I'll never forget the look on her face or the hurt in her voice when she said, "Could you be pregnant?"

I swore to her that I couldn't be, but she watched me like a hawk after that. I started to eat a bit more, and my weight crept back up to about 115 pounds. But it was a full nine months before my period returned.

We never called it anorexia, but that's exactly what it was. At the time, it was just a way of (not) eating that got me the results I wanted. And I certainly wasn't the only girl at school doing it. A few of my classmates were fueled mainly by the sugar in lollipops bought between class periods at the school store. One or two even slipped discreetly into the bathroom after lunch to stick their fingers down their throats. We wanted to maintain a certain body size, and to our teenaged minds, not eating seemed the most logical way to do it.

That kind of peer influence often plays a role in the development of eating disorders. Forty-year-old Colleen, mom to three daughters, remembers going on her first diet at twelve or thirteen, when she and her friends heard about the Scarsdale Diet, even though weight wasn't an issue for her.

"We heard about the diet, and back then, it just seemed like a good idea," she says. "But there was also pressure to be skinny. This was when all the after-school specials and books about anorexia were coming out. It was kind of an 'in' thing. I never wanted to be anorexic, but I kind of liked the attention that all these kids were getting. And it was the thing with my peers at the time as well. I actually had two friends from school who were hospitalized for anorexia. It was serious."

Sarah Maria, age twenty-nine, recovered from her own eating-disordered adolescence and is now a body image coach who runs a company called Break Free Beauty. By the end of her freshman year in high school, all of her friends were talking about dieting—although none of them were overweight, she says. She remembers a fellow student who lost a lot of weight between her freshman and sophomore years, and got a lot of attention for it. "I remember thinking, 'Wow, she looks great,'" Maria says. "I really wanted to be popular and liked, and somehow I made the instant correlation between thinness and popularity."

Maria says she went to the bookstore and got a couple of books about dieting. Soon, she was limiting herself to five hundred calories a day, even though she was active daily in sports. "That was kind of how it started," she says of her eating disorder. "There's something to be said for innocence because I really didn't think that was extreme."

That very innocence—and the lack of thinking about long-term consequences—is one of the things that's so scary for me as a mom when I think about girls and body image. After all, I didn't plan for my own eating disorder to happen. But when you're unhappy with your body and your teenage life, there's something incredibly powerful about the idea that you can change it. That feeling of power takes hold of you, and if your friends are doing it, too, it's all the more difficult to stop.

What Are Eating Disorders?

According to the National Eating Disorders Association (NEDA), eating disorders are potentially life-threatening conditions, not simply fad diets. Those who suffer from anorexia nervosa (often called anorexia) starve themselves and lose an excessive amount of weight, while those suffering from bulimia nervosa (often called bulimia) will binge eat and then use "compensatory behaviors" such as self-induced vomiting to undo the effects of their binge. Binge eating disorder is marked by recurrent food binges without the purging behavior seen in bulimia.

Currently, says the National Eating Disorders Association's "*2008 Fact Sheet on Eating Disorders*," nearly ten million females and one million males struggle with an eating disorder such as anorexia or bulimia, while millions more have binge eating disorder. Of the newly identified cases of anorexia, 40 percent are in girls ages fifteen to nineteen years old, with the peak onset of eating disorders occurring during puberty, according to NEDA.

Although eating disorders typically begin with a preoccupation with food and weight, they're often fueled by other factors such as low self-esteem, feelings of inadequacy or lack of control, and a history of being teased or ridiculed based on size or weight, says NEDA. Culture can also play its part, adding pressure by valuing thinness and an idealized version of the "perfect" body, and by emphasizing physical appearance over other qualities and strengths.

In a culture where thinner is better, it's no wonder so many girls go to such extreme methods to get and keep weight off. Sophie, age fifteen, who weighs about ninety pounds because of a health issue that makes it hard for her to gain weight, bristles when people assume she has an eating disorder. Still, she acknowledges that her thin frame is the envy of many girls her age. "My two best friends constantly tell me they would kill for my body. I act like it's no big deal because I don't want to make them feel bad or anything, but it does make me happy to hear that," she says.

Karin, now forty-eight, says her eating disorder started shortly after she began dating the young man who'd eventually become her husband. She was in love, she says, and the weight seemed to melt off. Soon, she started getting compliments on her weight loss, so she just kept going. "I can honestly say I was on my way to anorexia," she says. "I'd have a cup of black coffee in the morning, and I wouldn't eat until he picked me up from work. I'd have a salad at about 10 at night."

That's all she would eat—all day long. She'd exercise morning and night for about an hour. More and more people started noticing the weight loss, and even her mother complimented her on the newly developed muscle tone in her legs.

"I remember weighing myself one morning in August," she says. "I weighed 121 pounds, and I thought, 'Wow, one more pound and I'll be 120.' But I also felt like I was going to die. My insides hurt so bad. Eventually, my sensibilities kicked in, and I told myself, 'You have to eat.'"

It's hard to talk about eating disorders without talking about the issue of control—not only over your physical body but also over your life. Body changes aren't the only major changes facing adolescent girls. There's also

more and harder schoolwork. There are changing relationships with friends. There's dating and worries about
capturing—or not capturing—the interest of boys. There
are drugs, alcohol, and pressure to do things they might
not be ready for. For some girls, adolescence also coin-
cides with bigger problems like the death of a parent or a
divorce. Some girls who develop eating disorders aren't
necessarily driven by the desire to be thin. Instead,
they're trying to find some place—*any place*—where they
can be completely in control, and for some, control becomes about what they do, or don't, put in their mouths.

Right now, at age thirteen, Faith is a healthy eater at
a healthy weight—as are most of her friends. But as
their bodies change, I know that at least one of these
girls will start to hate the way she looks and may flirt
with the idea of controlling her weight by not eating or
by purging. As moms, what can we do to help prevent
our daughters from going down the path of disordered
eating? And will we know the signs if we see them?

Talking to Your Daughter about Eating Disorders

Because eating disorders are often wrapped up in control
issues, talking with your daughter about them—especially
if you think she may have one—can be particularly tricky.
If you're simply looking to let her know the dangers of eating disorders or to find out how she feels about them, start

by educating yourself about what eating disorders are so that you can have an informed conversation. Then, consider using the experiences of a celebrity or someone you both know as a starting point—just as you did when teaching her how to think critically about media images. Making the conversation about a third party—as in an actress who is rumored to have an eating disorder—lets you introduce the subject in a way that won't be perceived as an accusation or criticism by your daughter. Ask her if she knows what anorexia and bulimia are; if she's open to talking, you can gently ask if she's seen any of her friends acting this way. This is also a great time to talk about peer influences and how going along with the crowd isn't always the best idea.

If you're worried that your daughter may be developing an eating disorder, it's more important than ever to keep your emotions in check. Let her know you're there to listen openly about what's going on and do everything you can not to judge what she tells you. If she's struggling, let her know that you love her and that you're her ally. Threatening, blaming, or making her feel guilty about her behavior may cause her to rebel against your attempts to control her or to simply shut you out completely.

Choosing Your Battles

Because of her own experience, Colleen is watching her daughters carefully for signs of bad body feelings. "It's just starting a little bit with my thirteen-year-old," she tells me. "Up until this year, she's always been very happy with her body. But now she's really into wearing Abercrombie and Hollister, and those clothes are really made for sticks. I noticed her stomach showing in some of these shirts, and I'll say, 'Maybe you need a bigger size' or 'That's not flattering for your body.' She gets upset, and she doesn't like it. Who would? But she's started to make comments about her physical appearance, and she's starting to talk about food and calories."

It can be really tough to bite your tongue when your daughter's wearing something that isn't flattering to her figure, but unless her clothes are completely inappropriate, biting your tongue is exactly what Sarah Maria advises. "Clothing is really a loaded thing," she says. "I can remember going shopping with my mom and feeling like there's more approval if I can fit into a smaller size."

According to the National Eating Disorders Association (NEDA), if you suspect your daughter may be developing an eating disorder, it's best to avoid situations where the main focus is on appearance, such as clothes shopping. It's also important not to emphasize the value of being at a certain weight or a certain size.

Appearance-based "suggestions" can also tap into the rebellious, pouty, "you're not the boss of me" nature of adolescent girls—another side of the control issue that often plays into the development of eating disorders. Nancy, age forty-one, says her fashionable mother was always dressed to the nines, while she purposely went in the other direction.

"I was always the queen of sweatpants," she says. "And my mother was always like, 'Don't you want to put a little makeup on?' We're very different people, and I didn't emulate her; in fact, in many ways, I fought against her."

But clothing and makeup weren't the only means Nancy used to rebel against her mom, who—having been a heavy teenager herself—was rigid and controlling about what Nancy and her sister ate. "We became secret eaters," she tells me. "We would sneak frozen bread slices from the freezer. We'd stuff jars of peanut butter into the couch downstairs when nobody was around. I started to gain weight, and it just triggered something more unhealthy as I started to eat more."

Some girls assert their independence and control by doing the opposite of what their mom does. Rachel, age forty-nine, is extremely active with her husband but has a hard time getting her three daughters to get up and move—and she's convinced that it's their idea of rebellion. "It's all I can think of because in every other way, they really aren't rebellious," she says. "They know I'm not going to make them do anything, so when I make myself heard, they just blow me off. It's almost like they've made a decision that they don't want to be like us."

We've all heard the parenting advice about "picking your battles." It's something I try to practice regularly with Faith. Does it really matter if she wears an outfit I don't think looks good, as long as it's not inappropriate for the occasion? Does it matter if she doesn't want to eat all her vegetables at dinner, as long as she's taking a multivitamin? Does it matter if she stays up reading later than I think she should, as long as she gets up for school in the morning and doesn't have trouble concentrating? By letting go of the small things and giving her some sense of control and independence, I hope that I'm empowering her enough that she won't feel she has to assert control through her eating and exercise habits. I also know I'll be able to put my foot down when the issue really matters.

Walking a Fine Line

"My eating habits are all over the place. I think my mom might be a little paranoid about eating disorders. When parents try to control our lives, we're even more encouraged to rebel against it. Only if things get dire should you try to step in and run our bodies for us."—Grace, age fifteen

There's definitely a line between healthy behavior and the beginnings of disordered eating. The key is to watch our daughters—and ourselves—for clues that we may be getting too close to that line. Of course we want our girls to take care of their bodies by eating healthy foods and exercising. But how do we encourage that without pushing too hard or creating an obsessive focus on food, calories, and weight control?

Watch your words.

It starts, first and foremost, with what we say—about ourselves and about them. Sarah Maria says that she was always the smallest-boned person in her family and her mother would often comment on how petite she was. "It created this sense in me that I really needed to be petite and small," she says. "There were a lot of subtle things like that that were really influential. It kind of set up an unrealistic standard for the weight I wanted to keep my body at."

Make sure she's not losing too much weight.

It's particularly difficult, I think, in situations like the one from my adolescence. I *was* overweight, and I *was* unhappy, so when my mother saw me losing weight and feeling better about myself, why would she want to stop me? For my mother, too, I think there was an element of pride that I could have the kind of high school experience that she felt she never had because she lacked confidence in herself and her body.

Maria knows a bit about that feeling, too. "When I did lose a lot of weight, my mom never said, 'This needs to stop,'" she says. Her father, who struggled with his own weight, often complimented her while she was losing weight—even though she didn't need to, she says. "That was a reflection of his own challenges," she tells me. "But it still made me think, 'OK, the thinner, the better.'"

Praise health, not weight loss.

It's all right to comment on the healthy choices your daughter is making, she says, but make your praise about the choices themselves—not the results of the choices, such as weight loss or wearing a smaller size. Eating disorders are very much about control; our daughters need to learn that we can control the choices we make, such as what we eat and how we exercise, but we can't control our bodies themselves—nor should we try.

Be a role model.

Of all the areas where moms serve as role models for their daughters, this idea of exactly how much control we have over how our bodies look is one of the most powerful. "Children model what they see their parents doing," Maria says. If you constantly make negative comments about your body, talk about losing weight, or praise others for losing weight, your daughter is likely to think that being thin is what you value most. And since most girls really want their mother's approval, this sort of dynamic sets up a situation that's ripe for the development of an eating disorder.

Just as important as what we say, however, is what we do. By nine or ten, most kids have figured out that adults may say one thing but do another. She needs to see you eat a healthy amount of food and exercise in a healthy way; if you're obsessively counting calories, stepping on and off the scale multiple times each day, or hitting the gym for both a morning and an afternoon workout, you aren't controlling your weight. It's controlling you—and she knows it.

Old Habits, New Generation

I was a bit nervous at the start of the Weight-Loss Diary column because I knew that Faith would be watching my weight-loss process every step of the way. Would my old adolescent mentality kick in and have me soon skipping meals and eating less and less, just to see results? I knew, too, that older women aren't immune to eating disorders; in fact, the Eating Disorder Center of Denver released a study in 2008 showing that more women between the ages of thirty and sixty-five were seeking treatment for eating disorders than ever before.[1] For some, the disorders developed later in life, often as a response to a stressful event, like divorce. But for many others, the study said, midlife eating disorders were a result of a relapse of an earlier eating disorder.

I'll be honest: I was afraid of that scenario. It's *in* me to be extremely disciplined and controlled, and the structured program of the Weight-Loss Diary column was all about control. Add to that the pressure of losing weight publicly, and I knew I was setting myself up for a potential relapse.

Fortunately, it didn't happen. My dietitian, Melissa, was great about teaching me—and Faith, whenever she was around to listen—about the scientific principles behind healthy weight loss. Still, I worried about how my focus on weight, pounds, and the scale would affect Faith. As I celebrated each pound lost—and people we barely knew congratulated me for shrinking before their eyes—would she come to think that thinner is automatically better? As my body was getting smaller and she began to put on the normal weight necessary to take her from girl to woman, would she think that I thought less of her? Worse, would she think her normal weight gain is something that needs to be "addressed" as her mom was addressing her own weight? I didn't want my weight-loss experience to be the initial push that started my daughter down a path of body loathing and diet obsession.

Because I was so concerned, I took every opportunity I could to talk to her about how I was eating more now than I ever had in the past—just different kinds of food. We also talked about how not eating enough food affects your body, making your hair fall out and your nails crack. I told her about my experience with disordered eating and how I once almost passed out in geometry class because I was so weak. At Christmastime, I'll confess I even used Karen Carpenter's lovely version of "I'll Be Home for Christmas" as a chance to talk about what happens when trying to control your weight goes too far.

If You Suspect She Has an Eating Disorder

If your daughter loses a few pounds, you don't necessarily have to panic and assume the worst. But do keep a lookout for some of these signs of a possible eating disorder (according to the National Eating Disorders Association):

- She talks—or thinks—about weight loss, calories, exercise, etc. constantly.
- She eats in a rigid or ritualistic way (moves food around on her plate, will eat only vegetables, etc.).
- She exercises excessively, even when she's tired or sick.
- She refuses to eat in public.
- She suddenly begins dressing in baggy clothes or lots of layers.
- She hoards, steals, or hides food.
- She makes frequent trips to the bathroom, and/or you see evidence of vomiting.
- She uses mouthwash or gum excessively, or has staining on her teeth.

If you suspect that she may have an eating disorder, gently share your concerns, and suggest that you make an appointment with a professional. Above all, make sure she knows that you love her and that you'll support her in working through this. If you're not sure of how to help your daughter, seek help for yourself from a professional, and consider joining a parent support group.

Carolyn, age forty-eight, learned some hard lessons about parenting when the oldest of her three daughters developed an eating disorder during her junior year of high school. She got some bad grades and was feeling really anxious about school. "She was having a bad year, and she was feeling isolated," she tells me. "The whole thing just kind of snowballed. She got stomachaches a lot, and she lost weight. I got pretty concerned when she saw a doctor over the summer—she had lost about twenty pounds—and he said she'd lost six pounds in the last two weeks."

She had to put "logical consequences" into place, she says, because the whole family was getting wound up by her daughter's eating—or not eating.

"People were reporting, 'She had a bagel for breakfast,'" she says. "It was ridiculous. The whole entire family was focused on what *she* had for breakfast and that was giving her a lot of secondary gains. So I flat-out said to her, 'You have an eating problem, and we can fix it. This is the way it's going to be. We're not going to let your eating problem be something that influences your sisters because I have an obligation to them, too.' I went to counseling with her for six months. The counselor was a really good therapist and was really respectful of my daughter. Over time, all this stuff came out, and she started eating again and gaining weight. But my daughter losing all that weight was the scariest thing I've ever been through in my whole life. You can't make them eat."

Cindy, age thirty-seven, tells me she wishes she'd learned not to "medicate" herself with food when things weren't going right in her life. "Eating isn't really the way to feel better," she says. "Your friends may be mad at you, and you're upset, or your mom just yelled at you. Eating makes you feel good momentarily, but you have to find another way to face it."

As moms, we need to stay aware of the fact that sometimes our girls are simply looking for a bit of control over their lives. Talk to your daughter about what she's feeling, and if she's overwhelmed, there's no shame in seeking professional help. A good therapist can help her understand why she's behaving the way she is and help her develop coping strategies that don't have anything to do with eating. Call your health insurance provider, or contact a local hospital for help with finding a therapist or support group. You can also find additional resources at www.nationaleatingdisorders.org.

Learning to Trust Your Body

While it's true that some girls emulate the disordered eating behavior of others—whether they're friends, sisters, cousins, or even moms—some girls see those experiences as cautionary. That's how it was for forty-five-year-old Maggie, mom to a fourteen-year-old daughter. "I was the youngest of five girls, and two of my older sisters were very critical of their bodies," she says. "Through them, I saw what anorexia and bulimia did. My mom talked to me about my sisters' negative behavior, and she definitely discouraged it."

Ironically, there's a calming sense of order that comes from letting go of the need to control your body and learning to trust it instead.

As an adult, Maggie says she doesn't diet, but she does focus on cooking healthy meals with her daughter and exercising together. "I work out to be strong and to maintain a healthy weight. We do compare our body parts, like our hair and our muscles and our dimples," she says. "I don't think my daughter has any concerns about her body. She feels good about the way she looks. I hope that I've passed on a healthy body image to her."

Maggie's relaxed approach to weight control is a great example for her daughter. Modeling healthy eating and exercise behavior is important, but so is modeling an accepting attitude. When we let go of the need to try to rigidly control our bodies and simply accept who we are, we help our daughters to do the same.

Body Image Builders

Sometimes, body dissatisfaction goes way too far, crossing the line into eating disorders and unhealthy obsession. Here's what to do to set a healthy example and help keep eating disorders at bay:

Conquer your own demons. If you've got an eating-disordered past and feel yourself slipping back into old habits, the time to address it is now. Talk to a doctor, a therapist, or a trusted friend. It's not just about you and your health—it's also about the example you're setting for your daughter.

Give up some control. If your parenting style tends to be rigid and controlling, easing up a bit where it doesn't matter will let your daughter feel assertive, independent, and more in control of her own life.

Talk; don't eat. When problems arise or you're feeling stressed out, don't bury your feelings in food. Talk it out, or take a walk. Let her see you handling your emotions without food.

Keep your eyes open. While you don't want to control everything she eats, do make sure that she's eating. Moving food around on her plate, creating rigid rules or rituals for eating, and pretending she's full may be early signs of a problem.

Know her friends. Because peers can influence dieting behavior and the development of eating disorders, make sure you know who she's hanging around with. If you notice her friend starting to get thinner, talk to your daughter about what's going on with her pal.

12

If I'd Only Known Then . . .
Reflections on Body Image

> You're only as beautiful as you think you are, so
> you can't be pretty unless you learn that you're
> pretty. People come in all shapes and sizes, and
> you have to deal with the one you've been given.
>
> —*Amanda, age thirteen*

Faith and I often sit down together and watch TV makeover shows; we love to sit on the couch on a Friday night and catch back-to-back episodes of *What Not to Wear*. It's always thrilling to watch somebody be transformed—especially when the camera captures that moment where they see themselves for the first time. You can almost read their thoughts: "Now, things will be different."

But guess what? Things aren't always so different.

It's a point I learned firsthand at the end of my year writing the Weight-Loss Diary column. Though I'd reached and surpassed my goal weight, it wasn't as if I snapped my fingers and my body was suddenly perfect. Twenty-six fewer pounds didn't magically erase years of feeling bad about my body. But the yearlong journey of taking the weight off did help me reach the life-changing moment I'd been seeking: that *this* body was the best body I could be in right now. It's still not a perfect body; it's not even the same body I had at twenty-five, although my weight is the same. It's *this* body at *this* time in my life—and it's good enough.

Say it with me now: My *body is good enough.*

I know it's easy to say and not always so easy to believe. But here's the thing—by saying it, and doing our best to live as if it were true, we may just find that it does become something believable for us. As Pavitra Ciavardone, my life coach for the Weight-Loss Diary column, used to tell me, our words become our reality.

Though it was one of the hardest things I've ever done, writing the Weight-Loss Diary was so much more than just a chance to lose some weight. More than anything, it was an opportunity to show my kids how much better you can feel when you take care of your health. But I also knew that the most important body image example I'd set for them—especially for my daughter—would come not during the project, but rather, when it was over. All along, I'd been telling Faith that I was doing this to be healthy and to be the best "me" I could be. When the column ended, it was time to put up or shut up—there could be no more picking my body apart, pointing out the remaining flaws, or otherwise berating myself. If I did that, the message would no longer be about making the most of what you are. It would be that no matter how hard you work and how much effort you put in, you're still not good enough.

That's a message I know I don't want to send.

I learned a lot about the human body when I was writing that column. I learned that the right foods—at the right time—really can have a big effect on your appearance and your attitude. I learned that exercise improves not only how you look, but also how you think and feel. I learned that the scale is not a reliable measure of good health—or a reflection of your virtue. And I learned that no matter how hard you work, at a certain point, your body *is what it is.*

For me and for my merry band of fellow perfectionists, that's a truly life-changing discovery. Simply put, learning to let go of what can't be changed opens the door to acceptance.

And yet a woman's body is constantly changing. At puberty, you leave girlhood behind and become a young woman. In adulthood, many of us confront the changes that our bodies go through when we give birth to children and become mothers. Now, at forty, I know I'll soon be facing more body changes as I look ahead to menopause. The body I have today isn't the body I'll have next year. There's no finish line where it will suddenly be perfect.

Learning to love my body—and teaching my daughter to love hers—is about meeting and accepting it, *this* body, where it is today.

As I write this chapter, I've just finished a magazine piece on how a woman's body image changes over time. In it, I offered tips from experts on how women can learn to live with the changes they're seeing as they get older. Though they said it in different ways, all of the experts I talked to noted that getting older gives women a certain freedom from outside expectations, and all of them mentioned the importance of giving yourself permission to feel good about your body, just the way it is.

The very word "permission" implies that the power has been ours all along. At the risk of sounding too much like Glinda the Good Witch from *The Wizard of Oz*, the power to accept my body as it is has always been mine. I chose to give it away, just as my mom did.

And I want something different for my daughter.

A New Appreciation

I was fully committed to making my weight loss happen while I was writing the Weight-Loss Diary. I bought into it mind, body, and soul, telling myself that I was doing this not only to feel better about the way I looked and set a good body example for my daughter, but also to drop weight that might cause health problems as I got older. Now I find it laughable that what pushed me over goal weight in the end was a violent illness that landed me in the hospital.

I can laugh at it now. But I sure wasn't laughing then.

After a couple of days of high fever and chronic diarrhea, I spent three scary days in the hospital thinking I might have cancer or Crohn's disease, an inflammatory bowel disease that can be debilitating and life-threatening and, ironically, causes extreme weight loss. X-rays, a CAT scan, a colonoscopy—I had it all, and I was downright terrified.

As I lay in my bed crying in the late-afternoon hours, a very nice nurse came in and sat down on the edge of my bed. "What's going on?" he asked.

"I'm really, really scared," I told him.

As he tried to reassure me and explain how everything would be OK, I wanted to scream at the poor guy. He had no idea what he was dealing with. How could he possibly know that what scared me most was that I'd wasted all those years of my life worrying about a body that was maybe a little too curvy but always healthy? I'd been so busy fretting about what I looked like in my bathing suit that I failed to appreciate a body that was strong enough to play in the waves with my children.

A few days later, I was feeling much better, and the doctor confirmed that my condition was, in fact, salmonella poisoning. I've never been so happy to have food poisoning! But as people I ran into congratulated me on my weight loss and told me how good I looked, I knew the truth: I could never let pounds be that important to me again.

Sometimes I like to think about how I want my kids—and, hopefully, my grandkids someday—to remember me. Not in a morbid way, but in a way that reminds me to stop and think about the long-term impact of what I say and do. Do I want them to remember me as someone who was always so worried about gaining weight that she wouldn't have an ice-cream cone with the family? Or do I want them to remember me as someone who was always up for fun, confident in her abilities, willing to stand up and speak out when necessary, and actively engaged with them and with the world around her?

Body image can affect all those things.

My mother once attended a "She and Me" Girl Scout breakfast with Faith and me. A photographer had been hired for the day to take portraits of all the mothers and daughters together. I tried to talk her into getting in the photo; in fact, I think I outright begged. I wanted a picture of our three generations together. But she refused; she hated being photographed because she didn't like the way she looked, so only Faith and I were in the picture that day. Three months later, my mother was dead. And when the photographs came back later that fall, I cried. That opportunity was gone forever, all because my mother didn't like to have her body captured on film.

I swear I think about that every time somebody wants to take my picture now. And though I may be momentarily tempted to refuse or turn away, I always take a deep breath, smile big, and turn my face right toward that camera. I want my kids to be able to look back at their mom someday and remember me as happy and confident.

When I look at the few pictures I have of my mother, I don't see the flaws that she thought the rest of the world saw. Since they were usually snapped in an unguarded moment, I see her as I remember her: laughing, smiling, saying something funny, holding my babies— as the mother and friend I loved so much.

Karin, age forty-eight, remembers her mother not as the big woman she appeared to be but as the big-hearted mom that she was. "When she got sick, she went down to about 160 pounds, and she said, 'I was always heavy, but thank goodness I had that extra weight,'" Karin tells me. "She had six kids, so over the years, she got bigger. But her arms around me were just so comforting. No hug ever felt as good as my mom's."

Part of the Journey

Certainly, losing a parent, sibling, or friend—or facing your own health crisis—gives you a whole new perspective on your body. It's hard to worry about jiggly thighs, chicken legs, or any of the other insults we regularly hurl at our bodies when you're just wishing for good health. Loving your body isn't about waiting until you've made it better—it's about accepting it for what it is *now* and making the most of what you have.

We may be there—or at least be on the road to getting there—but what about our daughters? Some might say it's a journey every woman has to take alone, but I profoundly disagree. My mother is no longer with me, but she's still in me—every step of the way. Just as I'll be with Faith.

It'd be great if we could simply say to our girls, "You're beautiful just the way you are," and they believed it. Can you imagine if it was that easy to spare them years of not feeling good enough?

Nancy, age forty-one, says she often has to fight the urge to grab her sons' girlfriends and tell them they're OK. "They're so sad," she says. "Their shoulders slouch when they walk. I look at them, and I think, 'You're so beautiful, you have no idea. Because you're not an emaciated size 2, you think you're fat?' I look at them, and I just cringe."

But it's not easy to talk somebody out of feeling bad about herself—words go only so far. It's impossible for us to completely insulate our girls against the influence of peers and boys and media images. The reality is that they will compare themselves to their friends. They will be hurt by something a boy says or does. And they will look at a magazine image and wonder, "Why can't I look like that?"

While we can't insulate, we can offer a buffer—and that buffer is our behavior toward our own bodies. Pavitra, age fifty-three, says that our words and behavior definitely have an impact on how our daughters feel about their bodies. When her daughter was a little girl, she says, her daughter witnessed her mother's drive to create a perfect appearance. "I made a lifelong habit of focusing on making my outside look good," she says. "I weighed myself every single day, and I was exercising all the time. I was always thinking, 'My thighs can be more toned,' or that I could tweak this or that. There was always something to improve."

Pavitra learned to put her need to be perfect aside when she learned to meditate—and taught her daughter to do the same. Rather than focusing on what you see in the mirror, meditation allows you to look at yourself on the inside, she says. "Meditation helped us both learn that we're not our bodies; our bodies are containers for who we are," she says. "If I had it all to do over, I'd have spent more time looking at what was inside—at the qualities of my heart rather than the shape of my legs."

While every woman has to take her own journey to self-acceptance, we can help our daughters along the way. "We can teach them how to say no and not feel guilty," she says. "My daughter saw me give so much of myself to other people. When I started to be gentle, nurturing, and kind to myself, I was able to maintain my weight easily. There was no more harshness or putting demands on my body. I became so comfortable with who I was inside that the outside didn't matter anymore."

Imagine, for one minute, how different our lives might look if we all took that attitude. Although Faith saw me work really hard at the gym during my year with *Shape*, now that it's over, I've let my gym membership lapse. I've realized it's not necessary to punish myself with grueling workouts to maintain my weight and keep myself healthy. Now I use a weight set and resistance bands at home for strength training, and I walk, take a dance class, or break out a workout DVD for my cardio. I'm still showing her that it's important to exercise, and I'm keeping my commitment to take care of my health. But I hope I'm also showing her that being healthy and feeling good about your body doesn't mean you have to be rigid or obsessive about it.

Wasted Time

It's hard to talk about my body image without thinking about all the time I've wasted judging myself harshly, berating myself for not measuring up to some standard, or denying myself the chance to do something or get to know someone because I didn't feel good about how I looked. Even as I write the words, just thinking about it makes me feel so shallow and petty. But I know I'm not the only woman who's felt this way.

"I'm very self-conscious at times and probably haven't done a lot of things because of that," Susan, age forty-four, tells me. "I've been happy with my body at other times, and when I'm not, I'm ashamed to admit that I'm ashamed of it. I'm ashamed that I'm so shallow that it matters and that I'm actually cringing each time I pass a mirror."

Susan's frustration and guilt are pretty common among the women I talked to for this book. There's a sense that how we feel about the way we look just shouldn't be so important. And the fact that so many of us have allowed feeling bad about our bodies to keep us from doing things we wanted or needed to do only adds to the feeling that we've wasted too much of our lives hating ourselves. I remember my mother once telling me wistfully, "If I could back knowing what I know now, I'd have done so many things differently."

I Wish I'd Known . . .

. . . that I didn't have to worry so much.

Pam, age forty-five, mom to twelve-year-old Allison, says she remembers looking at a video made for her when she turned forty. "It had all my pictures through the years," she says. "I always felt so big and was even referred to as big, but I wasn't really that big, ever. I look at how skinny I was and remember that I thought I was huge. I should have had more confidence and flaunted my stuff."

Pam says she doesn't want Allison to waste as much time as she did worrying about her looks. She also wants Allison to remember her as a mom who wasn't hung up on what she looked like and, instead, just enjoyed life. "Allison always wants me to go swimming with her," she tells me. "And I remember how much fun it was when my mom went in the water with us. So now I just sort of do an out-of-body experience and pretend I look great."

That's the thing about "acting as if." Before long, Pam says, she forgets that she's self-conscious about the way she looks in a bathing suit and just has a great time swimming with her daughter. Not only has she changed things for herself, but she's also changed the dynamic for Allison, who'll always remember that her mother felt comfortable enough with her body to jump right in the pool with her instead of sitting covered up on the sidelines. You might not think that simple changes in our own behavior would make such a difference to our girls, but they do.

. . . that I don't need the mirror.

Rachel, age forty-nine, also uses a unique tactic when it comes to setting a body image example for her three daughters: She doesn't spend a whole lot of time looking in the mirror.

"It's not that I'm unhappy with my face or body, but I find that I'm happier if I don't spend too much time looking at it," she tells me. "I totally accept who I am. Each of us has a special look, something that sets us apart. None of us is perfect, but if you don't love and accept yourself, you'll be thwarted in your attempts to love and accept others. These are mature concepts, but maybe if girls hear them at an early age repeatedly, they'll learn to believe it."

Rachel's nonchalant attitude toward her appearance has definitely rubbed off on at least one of her daughters.

"I'm pretty immodest like her," says her fifteen-year-old daughter, Sophie. "I think the fact that she doesn't care who sees if she changes clothes in the middle of the kitchen shows she's very comfortable with herself."

Learning to "get comfortable" with yourself does seem to get easier with time. But when you're fourteen and your body is changing, it's tough to look in the mirror each day and find something to love. It's so much easier to find the flaws. It's tough, too, to recognize that you're not the only one feeling this way. When Faith gets frustrated with the way she looks, I try to gently remind her that everybody has something about herself that she'd like to change.

That's what thirty-five-year-old Traci wishes she had known at thirteen.

. . . that everyone is insecure.

"I wish I'd known that I wasn't the only one insecure about my body," she says. "Everyone, from the most popular cheerleader to the smartest girl in the class, had the same doubts about their bodies. I thought that since I felt inferior, it meant I was inferior. If I had known everyone else out there was feeling the same way, I would have known I was normal."

In many ways, helping your daughter learn to love her body—and yourself to love your own—is about changing what's normal. As women, we're so conditioned to point out our flaws that it seems almost wrong not to do it. Many of us are uncomfortable accepting a compliment, and complimenting ourselves feels like an impossible task. But it's these subtle changes that will create an entirely new normal. It's not our bodies that need to change. It's how we treat them and speak about them.

Time and again, I replay my mother's mantra in my mind: "If you think you're fat, you are." Wherever she is now, I know she'll appreciate this: You were right, Mom.

What I couldn't grasp back then was that she was trying to tell me that it's what we tell ourselves about our bodies that creates our reality—and I now know it creates a reality for our daughters, too. By treating ourselves well, we change the body image blueprint we give to our girls. Instead of teaching them that our bodies are something to be molded and changed through obsessive dieting and exercise habits, we can show them that our bodies are worthy of care through healthy eating and exercise that make sense for us. We can show them that when we take good care of ourselves, we can be proud of the body we have and speak kindly about it—and speak kindly about others, too.

───────

Riding home from softball recently, I told Faith that I was wrapping up writing the book and jokingly asked her if she had any body image words of wisdom with which I could end. She thought for a minute, then said seriously, "I think body image is what you say to yourself and what you show to the world."

My father turned seventy a couple of weeks ago, and we invited a bunch of friends and relatives to come and mark the occasion. That afternoon, a cousin of my mother's—whom I hadn't seen since her funeral—walked through the door, took one look at me, and stopped in her tracks.

"My God," she said. "You look so much like your mother."

Normally, I'd have been quick with a smart-alecky comment or self-deprecating joke. But this time, I chose to take her words as the compliment I'm sure they were intended to be.

So I smiled and said, "Thanks."

Body Image Builders

Teaching our daughters to love their bodies—and ourselves to love our own—is about learning to see ourselves with fresh eyes and a new perspective. Want to make peace with your body? Try these tactics:

Cultivate kindness. When you're tempted to criticize—yourself or somebody else—stop and think for a moment. Is the criticism really necessary? Instead, try focusing on something positive.

Skip the mirror. OK, I'm not advocating leaving the house without a glance at yourself. But once you've done that, resist the urge to constantly recheck your look in mirrors, store windows, or any other reflective surface. You know you look fine, so just let the obsession go.

Appreciate your strengths. It's easy to find things you don't like about your body, but try focusing on what's right instead. I made my son feel my "guns" after I brought in six heavy bags of groceries the other night, and Faith and I often compare bicep muscles.

Revisit history together. Sit with your daughter, and flip through photographs of the women in your family. Compliment the people you see, and remind her of what a strong, loving family she comes from.

Notes

Chapter 4: Mom's Got Game

1. The Tucker Center for Research on Girls and Women in Sport, "Executive Summary," *The 2007 Tucker Center Research Report: Developing Physically Active Girls: An Evidence-based Multidisciplinary Approach,* University of Minnesota, Minneapolis, 2007, http://cehd.umn.edu/tuckercenter/projects/TCRR/executive-summary.html.

2. "Sports, Fitness and Women's Health," Women's Sports Foundation, November 1, 2000, http://www.womenssportsfoundation.org/Content/Articles/Issues/Body-and-Mind/S/Sports-Fitness-and-Womens-Health.aspx.

Chapter 5: Am I More if I'm Less?

1. "NWCR Facts," National Weight Control Registry, 2008, http://www.nwcr.ws/Research/default.htm.

Chapter 6: If I Looked Like Her, I'd Be Happy

1. Anita Gurian, PhD, "How to Raise Girls with Healthy Self-Esteem," NYU Child Study Center, http://www.aboutourkids.org/articles/how_raise_girls_healthy_selfesteem.

2. "Predictors of Media Effects on Body Dissatisfaction in European American Women," *Sex Roles: A Journal of Research,* March 2007, http://munews.missouri.edu/news-releases/2007/0326-body-dissatisfaction.php.

3. Hayley Dohnt and Marika Tiggemann, "The Contribution of Peer and Media Influence to the Development of Body Satisfaction and Self-Esteem in Young Girls: A Prospective Study," *Development Psychology* 42, no. 5 (September 2006): 929–36.

Chapter 7: Mean Girls and Frenemies

1. Allison G. Dempsey and Eric A. Storch, "Relational Victimization: The Association between Recalled Adolescent Social Experiences and Emotional Adjustment in Early Adulthood," *Psychology in the Schools* 45, no. 4 (April 2008): 310–22, ERIC #EJ788482, http://www.eric.ed.gov.

2. "'Club 21' Only for Thin, Pretty Girls," *Courier Mail,* April 22, 2008, http://www.news.com.au/adelaidenow/story/0,22606,23579542-5006301,00.html.

3. J. Kevin Thompson et al., "Relations among Multiple Peer Influences, Body Dissatisfaction, Eating Disturbance, and Self-Esteem: A Comparison of Average Weight, At Risk of Overweight, and Overweight Adolescent Girls," *Journal of Pediatric Psychology* 32, no. 1 (January/February 2007): 24–29, http://pt.wk health.com.

Chapter 9: The X(Y) Factor:
Boys, Brothers, Dads, and Husbands

1. Beth M. Levy, "Behavior Problems: Name-Calling and Teasing: Information for Parents and Educators," National Association of School Psychologists, 2004; http://www.nasponline.org/resources/handouts/revisedPDFs/namecalling.pdf; reprinted from

Helping Children at Home and School II: Handouts for Families and Educators, National Association of School Psychologists, 2004.

2. Anita Gurian, PhD, "How to Raise Girls with Healthy Self-Esteem," NYU Child Study Center, http://www.aboutour kids.org/articles/how_raise_girls_healthy_selfesteem.

Chapter 10: Success Is for Skinny Girls

1. William J. Cromie, "Faking Happiness for Fun and Profit: Study: Smile and World Smiles Back," *Harvard Gazette*, January 23, 2003, http://www.hno.harvard.edu/gazette/2003/01.23/13 -smile.html.

Chapter 11: When Body Image Goes All Wrong

1. Sheryl Bass, "The Desperate Housewives Result: First Scientific Study Reveals Growing Population Suffer from Eating Disorders in Midlife," Eating Disorder Center of Denver, February 28, 2008, http://www.mednews.com/eating-disorders-women.

Resources

If you'd like more information on some of the topics discussed in this book, the following resources may be helpful.

Body Image

Books

Goldman, Leslie. *Locker Room Diaries: The Naked Truth about Women, Body Image, and Re-imagining the "Perfect" Body*. Cambridge, MA: Da Capo Press, 2006.

Maine, Margo, and Joe Kelly. *The Body Myth: Adult Women and the Pressure to Be Perfect*. Hoboken, NJ: John Wiley, 2005.

Redd, Nancy Amanda. *Body Drama: Real Girls, Real Bodies, Real Issues, Real Answers*. New York: Gotham, 2007.

Websites

Boston Women's Health Book Collective: http://www.ourbodies ourselves.org

Butler Hospital Body Image Program: http://www.bodyimage program.com

Kaz Cooke's Completely Gorgeous: http://www.completely gorgeous.com

Jessica Weiner, author: http://www.jessicaweiner.com

Sarah Maria, body image expert: http://www.breakfreebeauty.com

Bullying

Books

Dellasega, Cheryl, and Charisse Nixon. *Girl Wars: 12 Strategies that Will End Female Bullying*. New York: Simon & Schuster, 2003.

Simmons, Rachel. *Odd Girl Out: The Hidden Culture of Aggression in Girls*. New York: Harcourt, 2003.

Wiseman, Rosalind. *Queen Bees and Wannabes: Helping Your Daughter Survive Cliques, Gossip, Boyfriends, and Other Realities of Adolescence*. New York: Crown, 2002.

Communication

Books

Cohen-Sandler, Roni, and Michelle Silver. *I'm Not Mad, I Just Hate You! A New Understanding of Mother-Daughter Conflict*. New York: Viking, 1999.

Tannen, Deborah. *You're Wearing That? Understanding Mothers and Daughters in Conversation*. New York: Random House, 2006.

Weiner, Jessica. *Do I Look Fat in This? Life Doesn't Begin Five Pounds from Now*. New York: Simon Spotlight Entertainment, 2006.

Eating Disorders

Books

Natenshon, Abigail. *When Your Child Has an Eating Disorder: A Step-by-Step Workbook for Parents and Other Caregivers*. San Francisco: Jossey-Bass, 1999.

Smeltzer, Doris. *Andrea's Voice—Silenced by Bulimia: Her Story and Her Mother's Journey through Grief toward Understanding.* Carlsbad, CA: Gurze Books, 2006.

Weiner, Jessica. *A Very Hungry Girl: How I Filled Up on Life—and How You Can, Too!* Carlsbad, CA: Hay House, 2003.

Websites

Abigail H. Natenshon, Empowered Parents: http://www.empoweredparents.com

The Emily Program: http://www.emilyprogram.com

National Eating Disorders Association: http://www.nationaleatingdisorders.org

The Renfrew Center: http://www.renfrewcenter.com

Fathers and Daughters

Books

Kelly, Joe. *Dads and Daughters: How to Inspire, Understand, and Support Your Daughter When She's Growing Up So Fast.* New York: Broadway Books, 2002.

Maine, Margo. *Father Hunger: Fathers, Daughters, and the Pursuit of Thinness.* 2nd ed. Carlsbad, CA: Gurze Books, 2004.

Websites

Dads and Daughters: http://www.thedadman.com/dadsanddaughters

Healthy Eating

Books

Bartell, Susan S. *Dr. Susan's Girls-Only Weight Loss Guide: The Easy, Fun Way to Look and Feel Good.* New York: Parent Positive, 2006.

Hendel, Amy. *Fat Families, Thin Families: How to Save Your Family from the Obesity Trap*. Dallas: BenBella Books, 2008.

Jana, Laura A., and Jennifer Shu. *Food Fights: Winning the Nutritional Challenges of Parenthood Armed with Insight, Humor and a Bottle of Ketchup*. Washington, DC: American Academy of Pediatrics, 2008.

Neumark-Sztainer, Dianne. *I'm, Like, SO Fat! Helping Your Teen Make Healthy Choices about Eating and Exercise in a Weight-Obsessed World*. New York: Guilford Press, 2005.

Media Images of Girls and Women

Books

Brashich, Audrey D. *All Made Up: A Girl's Guide to Seeing Through Celebrity Hype and Celebrating Real Beauty*. New York: Walker & Company, 2006.

Kilbourne, Jean. *Deadly Persuasion: Why Women and Girls Must Fight the Addictive Power of Advertising*. New York: Free Press, 1999.

Websites

Dove Campaign for Real Beauty: http://www.campaignforreal beauty.com

Jean Kilbourne, author and documentary filmmaker: http://www.jeankilbourne.com

Sports and Exercise

Books

Fish, Joel, with Susan Magee. *101 Ways to Be a Terrific Sports Parent: Making Athletics a Positive Experience for Your Child*. New York: Simon & Schuster, 2003.

Gottesman, Jane. *Game Face: What Does a Female Athlete Look Like?* Edited by Geoffrey Biddle. New York: Random House, 2001.

Zimmerman, Jean, and Gil Reavill. *Raising Our Athletic Daughters: How Sports Can Build Self-Esteem and Save Girls' Lives.* New York: Doubleday, 1998.

Websites

Tucker Center for Research on Girls and Women in Sport, University of Minnesota: http://www.tuckercenter.org

Women's Sports Foundation: http://www.womenssportsfoundation.org

Acknowledgments

I usually read book acknowledgments with the skeptical eye of a journalist. Did all those people mentioned really play a role in the author's writing? Now that I know just how much time and effort goes into the creation of a book, I'll never ask that question again.

With that said, I'm truly grateful to the many women and girls who so generously shared their time and stories with me. I'm humbled by your honesty and your willingness to open your lives to me. All of you with whom I had contact have helped shape this book, and I thank you. Thanks, too, to the many people who forwarded emails and otherwise helped me find women who might like to share their story.

I'm grateful to my agent, Elisabeth Weed, for her enthusiasm for and belief in this book—and in me. Thank you, too, to the amazing Jennifer Lawler for helping me refine my ideas and for answering all my questions. Thanks, also, to my editor, Katie McHugh, for her thought-provoking comments and smart editing.

I'm grateful to the staff at *Shape* magazine and to my expert team—Pavitra Ciavardone, Nicole Couto, and Melissa Kirdzik. Thank you for the opportunity and for helping me rediscover the girl I was and the woman I am.

The life of a writer is a solitary one, and I'd be lost without my daily dose of FLX. I'm lucky to be part of such a wonderful group of smart, funny, giving, and talented writers. I'm particularly grateful to those of you who offered a word of encouragement, an introduction, or a much-needed laugh throughout this process, especially Allison Winn Scotch, Rachel Weingarten, Michele Wojciechowski, Lisa Palmer, and Kerri Fivecoat-Campbell.

Thanks, Dad, for being so proud of me and of this book. Your love and support mean the world to me. Thanks, too, to my brothers and their families for the love and laughs you've offered. Diane, I appreciate your support, too.

Julia, thanks for being like the sister I never had. All the walks, talks, reassurances, laughs, and "panic yourself into greatness" moments have meant more to me than I can ever express.

It's not easy being the child of a writer—you never know when something you feel or say is going to wind up as your mom's funny anecdote or illustrative point. I'm forever grateful to you, Faith, for allowing me to share so much of your life with my readers. You're beautiful in every way, and I'm grateful for the privilege of being your mom.

Evan, thanks for being such a cool and caring guy. You always know how to make me laugh and just when I need a hug. I couldn't have asked for a more fun job than being your mom.

Finally, every dreamer needs a solid foundation from which their loftiest aspirations can take off. Thanks, John, for always being my foundation and for never saying, "You're going to do what?" even though I'm sure you must be thinking it sometimes. I'm lucky to have you.

Index